A MINI COURSE
IN TRAINING DESIGN

A Mini Course in Training Design

*A Simple Approach to a
Not-So-Simple Subject*

William A. Welch Sr., EdD

iUniverse, Inc.
Bloomington

A Mini Course in Training Design
A Simple Approach to a Not-So-Simple Subject

iUniverse books may be ordered through booksellers or by contacting:

iUniverse
1663 Liberty Drive
Bloomington, IN 47403
www.iuniverse.com
1-800-Authors (1-800-288-4677)

ISBN: 978-1-4620-4661-4 (sc)
ISBN: 978-1-4620-4662-1 (hc)
ISBN: 978-1-4620-4663-8 (ebk)

Library of Congress Control Number: 2011914370

Printed in the United States of America

iUniverse rev. date: 08/24/2011

CONTENTS

To Kennedie and Tiffany
My Granddaughters
Who have brought so much light into my life
And
Who continue to be my teachers.
To my daughter Lyrica and my son Bill Welch, Jr.,
Who caused them to be and whom I also love
and respect.

INTRODUCTION
THE BOOK, IT'S FORMAT, AND FOR WHOM IT IS INTENDED

It has been said that everyone is involved in providing some form of learning. As parents, we decide on the learning needs of our charges and proceed to impart that learning over a specified period (for some of our offspring that period seems to extend for life).

Every supervisor is a teacher, whether or not he or she accepts the responsibility for carrying out that charge. We often teach by default; we fail to understand that we teach by the way we are observed by others. We are responsible for the development of those in our charge to the extent that they are able to pursue excellence in the areas of their responsibilities.

Ministers, priests, rabbis, and imams, to name a few of the religious leaders, are also concerned with providing learning, competencies necessary for the practice of the doctrines they are responsible for, along with a myriad of ancillary areas they are called upon to deliver. They are responsible for the training of their ministerial assistants as well as the congregations they lead.

The foregoing enumeration is by no means an exhaustive list of those who are in the training, education, and development practice, whether or not they realize the extent to which this is true. Suffice it to say that most persons could benefit from mastering techniques in assessing, designing, delivering, and evaluating learning experiences. It is also reasonable to assert that the overwhelming majority of those who would benefit do not have a great deal of time on their hands; thus whatever medium is available to assist them in developing these competencies must take this factor into account. Additionally, this medium must be able to be easily understood by those who do not have a comprehensive background in educational technology and at the same time provide worthy assistance to those who do. It is the writer's contentions that these challenges have been met by this book, and it is his hope that when you have completed your reading, you will agree.

The outline follows the steps in designing as practiced by many in the field and the writer in particular. It begins with the assessment of the needs to be fulfilled or problems to be resolved by the learning experience and proceeds to the constructing of performance objectives and activities to achieve the objectives and climate setting and to establishing the learning contract, evaluation, and closure. It will be quickly noticed that the actual delivery does not follow this sequence. Rather the flow of a session is generally as follows:

- *Activities to Establish the Learning Atmosphere.* (Sometimes this is preceded by introductions and housekeeping, where things are, house rules, etc. Sometimes the two are combined).
- *Establishing the Learning Contract.* Gaining agreement on what is to be learned, how it will be learned, and what standards or norms will be operative.
- *Activities to Achieve the Performance Objectives.* The presentation of activities that are designed to provide the learning experiences for which the session was organized.
- *Evaluation.* Activities to determine the effectiveness of the session and to encourage further learning.
- *Closure.* The redirection of energies from in-session learning to back-home application.

The reasons for the elements being treated out of the order in which they would be experienced in the session is explained in detail further in the text. Suffice it to say here that it is difficult to design an activity to establish the type of climate that would be best for a session for which the activities that the participants will be doing have not been designed. Said differently, how would the designer know what climate is appropriate unless he or she knew what the learners would be asked to do in the various modules?

Readability was considered a priority in the development of this book. A minimum of jargon is used in this publication, and that jargon found necessary is fully explained. Brevity was also a consideration. The writer suggests that the reader decide 1) what need he or she wishes to fulfill,

2) what problem he or she wishes to resolve that he or she feels reading this book will accomplish, and 3) what performance the reader wishes to enhance. The more specifically the needs or problems can be stated, the better the chance of achieving them. Keep them in mind as you read. In the end, evaluate your learning, apply what you have learned, and evaluate what you have learned again.

I
THEORY AND PRACTICES IN ADULT LEARNING

It is important and appropriate to begin our brief journey into the development of learning activities by exploring some of the basic fundamentals of adult learning. It is, after all, the adult population that we are primarily concerned about in this book. Additionally, "for the first time in our society, adults outnumber youths, there are more older adults, the population is better educated than ever before, and there is more cultural and ethnic diversity" (Merriam, Caffarella, & Baumgartner, 2007, p. 7). This change provides many opportunities and challenges. It provides opportunities to serve a vast market and challenges to design and deliver learning experiences to a complex mixture of clients whose needs are equally as diverse as they themselves are.

For decades, whenever the subject of adult learning has surfaced, one name immediately comes to mind: Malcolm Knowles. Synonymous with that name is the term *andragogy*. There is no single theory that explains all adult learning, although there have been and continues to be considerable effort directed toward that end. Knowles (1984; 1992; 1998) presented his concept of andragogy offering a difference between the learning styles and needs of children and adults. He describes the two approaches, pedagogy and andragogy, which in my view have also been misinterpreted as a dichotomy, an either/or approach to teaching, facilitating learning for children and adults. The word itself comes from the Greek words *paid*, meaning "child," and *agogus*, meaning "leader of," literally translated together meaning the art and science of teaching children (Knowles, Holton, & Swanson, 1998).

In the pedagogy approach the teacher decides what the learner needs to know and proceeds to develop and deliver the instruction designed to relieve the knowledge or skill deficiency. It is assumed that children have little if any experience that the teacher needs to consider in the teaching process. The assumption that the learner has little relevant knowledge of the subject being taught or any particularly relevant life experience that needs to be considered would create a real dilemma for anyone teaching adults. "To adults, their experience is who they are. In any situation in which adults' experience is ignored or devalued, they perceive this as not rejecting just their experience, but rejecting them as persons" (Knowles et al., p. 58). Horton and Freire (1990) insist that "you can't say you respect people and not respect their experiences" (p. 178).

After a brief review of the foregoing we come easily to the conclusion that there are situations in which adults need a pedagogical approach and children an andragogical approach. It is more about what the learner knows, his or her experience and or training in a given area, that controls the decision as to which approach is more suitable.

The andragogical approach does in fact take into account the experiences of the learner. It makes several assumptions about the learner, among them that they "have a self-concept of being responsible for their own decisions, for their own lives" (Knowles, et al., 1998, p. 65). Knowles offers additionally the following assumptions on which the andragogical model is based:

- Adults need to know why they need to know a particular thing or have a particular skill before they move to learn it.
- They become ready to learn in order to cope with real-life situations. Readiness, Knowles points out, is associated with moving from one developmental stage to another.
- They are life-centered in their orientation to learning in contrast with their youthful counterparts, who are more subject-centered oriented.
- Adults are motivated more by internal pressures, such as job satisfaction, self-esteem, and quality of life, than by external motivators, such as better jobs, promotions, or higher salaries.

It must be said at the outset that Knowles's assumptions have been seriously questioned by many, among them Brookfield (1996), Merriman, Mott, & Lee (1996), Hanson (1996), and Merriam, Cafferella, & Baumgartner (2007). In fact Brookfield questions whether andragogy is a theory at all. Perhaps the last word should be that of Knowles himself when he stated that he "prefers to think of [andragogy] as a model of assumptions about learning or a conceptual framework that serves as a basis for an emergent theory" (Knowles, 1989, p. 112).

One difficulty for some in using the andragogy/pedagogy continuum is where to place a particular adult on the continuum. After all, we know that most adults do not develop in all aspects at the same pace and thus may be quite self-directed about one set of responsibilities and far less self-directed in another. Additionally there are probably wide variations among the self-directedness of all of them. What tools can be utilized to make decisions as to the different levels of knowledge, experience, and motivation the learner brings to the session?

The SLII (Blanchard, Zigarmi & Zigarmi) model, for example, has two extremes and two points in between. The points regarding the development levels of the learner/follower are clearly identified at each level, which helps in deciding the needs of the learner as well as how to facilitate the learning experience. It provides a clear process by which persons may be led from incompetence to competence or from one level of competence to another by having solid cues as to when direction and/or support is needed and at what levels of intensity. It would be safe to assume that participants come to a learning session at differing levels of competence and motivation to learn and therefore are at different points on the andragogy/pedagogy continuum. The facilitator must then identify where the participants are and deal with them accordingly. The objective would be to assist them toward becoming self-directed human beings.

Adult Educators and Definitions of Adult Education

Included in the writer's concept of adult educator are those who teach adults in educational institutions, religious leaders, facilitators/trainers, supervisors, managers, or anyone who has as a job or volunteer responsibility for teaching adults. They are included because I believe that understanding basic fundamentals of adult learning is an indispensable part of the competency required for the work they must do. I believe also that it is important that we have a definition of adult education that we can ascribe to. I have accepted the view from Brookfield "as a dialogue among equals, an endeavor in cooperative learning" (1995, p. 208). I accept as well the position of Linderman, who gave the following definition of adult education: "A cooperative venture in nonauthoritarian, informal learning, the chief purpose of which is to discover the meaning of experience; a quest of the mind which digs down to the roots of the preconceptions which formulate our conduct" (Linderman, 1925, p. 3). He further insists that education "begins not with subject matter but with the situations and experiences which mold adult life . . . a method whereby the experiences and ideologies of adults are freed from traditional bonds" (p. 33).

Merriam, Caffarella, and Baumgartner (2007) provide what they term the main goals of adult learning: 1) to enhance the abilities of adult learners to be self-directed in their learning, 2) to foster transformational learning as central to self-directed learning, and 3) to promote emancipatory learning and social action as an integral part of self-directed learning.

Critical Reflection and Transformation Learning

Brookfield's (1995) position would appear be a precursor to Merriam, Caffarella, and Baumgartner (2007) and to flow directly from and directly support Linderman, whose words were written in the first quarter of the last century of the last millennium. "Teachers have a choice either to work in ways that legitimize and reinforce the status quo or in ways that liberate and transform the possibilities people see in their lives" (Brookfield, 1995, p. 209). Brookfield is one of the preeminent contributors to the adult learning theory of transformation learning and critical reflection, particularly in teaching. Critical reflection is "a critique of the presuppositions on which our beliefs have been built" (Mezirow, 1990, p. 1). Reflection becomes critical when it has two distinctive purposes: first, to understand how considerations of power undergird, frame, and distort the workplace processes and interactions; and second, to question assumptions and practices that seem to make our working lives easier but actually work against our long-term best interest (Mezirow,1990).

Mezirow (2000) defines learning as "the process of using a prior interpretation to construe a new or revised interpretation of the meaning of one's experience in order to guide future actions" (p. 5). We then have as our charge the responsibility of creating the opportunities for persons to revisit experiences, honestly question their present views, feelings, and assumptions about them, and conclude whether or not they still see them in the same light. So learning becomes a series of reinterpretations of our experiences. Such reinterpretations may well change how we see the world around us. This is what Cranton (1996) terms "the process of emancipatory learning—becoming free from forces that have limited our options, forces that have been taken for granted or as seen beyond our control" (p. 2). Transformative learning occurs when an individual has reflected on assumptions or expectations about what will occur, has found these assumptions to be faulty, and has revised them. They have transformed their way of viewing a particular premise (Cranton,1996; Mezirow, 1990).

In the workplace, we are constantly attempting to transform how persons not only perform but how they feel about work, processes, coworkers, and so on. Religious leaders have, among others, the tasks of changing how individuals see themselves and their concept of humankind in their relationship to God. The whole issue of diversity, from persons with challenging conditions to people who are racially different, requires us to seek changes in the way some see and behave toward others that are different. We are all involved in some kind of effort directed at some kind of transformation.

Much of how we see the world is greatly influenced by our meaning perspectives, which are primarily "uncritically acquired in childhood through the process of socialization, often in the context of an emotionally charged relationship with parents, teachers, or other mentors" (Mezirow, 1990, p. 3). Adulthood is the time for reassessing the assumptions of our formative years that have resulted in distorted views. We can help persons transform their meaning schemes through helping them reflect upon anomalies. As referenced before, these reinterpretations cover the gamut of our experiences. We learn to the extent that we are able to reflect upon our assumptions and behaviors and make determinations as to their fitness for us at a given moment. How we supervise subordinates, specific initiatives we have taken with them, or reactions we have had to them have all been subjected to our critical review from time to time and have sometimes resulted in our becoming better at supervising/leading people. Becoming skilled at helping others take better advantage of this method will help them learn more powerfully from their experiences throughout life.

William A. Welch Sr., EdD

On Becoming a Motivational Facilitator

Much is said about motivation in facilitating adult learning. How can I become a more motivating presenter? This question is continually raised. Motivation is an internal drive. I am of the view that while we cannot motivate persons, we may create an environment that is conducive for persons to act on their motivational tensions. We may also help create a realistic expectancy that making the necessary effort to achieve the outcome that they are motivated to seek is in fact a realistic one, thus making it more probable that the effort will be made.

Wlodkowski (1985) offers five critical assumptions for helping adults want to learn. In his first assumption he states that "people are always motivated" (p. 12). When we dismiss persons as not being motivated, he would insist that "it is more accurate to say, 'This learner is not motivated to learn with me'" (p. 12). We then are left with the problem of identifying the why of that condition and finding ways to overcome it. Wlodkowski further offers four of what he terms cornerstones on which he suggests our efforts to become a motivating instructor/teacher/facilitator can rest: *expertise, empathy, enthusiasm,* and *clarity.* He offers these as skills to be developed, not as traits or abstractions. He insists that they can be learned as other skills are learned.

Expertise

We certainly will not find any arguments against anyone being prepared, being thoroughly knowledgeable in their chosen fields. It also follows that it is this perception on the part of the learners of the instructor's competence that encourages them to at least pay attention, which allows the instructor to further engage them toward acting on their motivational tensions. It is important for us to critically evaluate how we demonstrate our expertise. If we have a presentation style that belies our level of knowledge or skill in a given area, we will not be perceived as having any.

Empathy

Certainly anyone working with adults needs to be understanding of the kinds of dilemmas, feelings, frustrations, issues, and fears many of the adult learners bring with them to the learning environment. How do we construct learning modules and develop presentation plans without this ability? How can we be sensitive to the various undercurrents so common in the learning environment? How do we become alert to the learner's needs? Without understanding their needs, we will not understand their reactions to what we present.

Schwarz (2002) offers a very important distinction regarding the conception of empathy/compassion. He asserts that compassion "is sometimes mistakenly thought of as having pity for others. Pity leads you to help protect others such that in the long run it is not helpful and leaves people less protected" (p. 88). Swartz goes on to say the best help is that which "enables you to have empathy for others and yourself while holding yourself and others accountable for action rather than unilaterally protecting others or yourself" (p. 88).

Wlodkowski (1985) points out that "adult needs and expectations for what they are taught will powerfully influence how they motivationally respond to what they are taught" (p. 23) The more their needs and expectations are met by what and how they learn, the more they will be motivated to learn. Conversely, the more often their needs and expectations are not met, the lesser the chances that they will be motivated to learn. Our group and individual management capabilities will be seriously deficient without strong empathic skills particularly of the type that Schwarz (2002) mentions in the preceding paragraph.

Enthusiasm

If you have ever heard or seen a truly great speaker or tuned in to one of the more popular evangelists, what comes across immediately is their enthusiasm for whatever they happen to be advocating. What comes through equally as strongly is the tremendous response they receive from their audiences. People are "up," interested, asking for more. Enthusiasm increases believability, signals a sense of commitment on the part of the facilitator, and enhances learner motivation. It causes people to pay attention, to listen. Once they begin to listen, most of the battle is won. Once they begin to feel it so is the war.

Clarity

Wlodkowski strongly advocates for instructional clarity. He defines instructional clarity as "teaching something in a manner that is easy for learners to understand and that is organized so that they can smoothly follow the intended lesson or program" (Wlodkowski, 1985, p. 40). He acknowledges that this is made difficult to do in that what is understood by one may well not be understood by another. Asking for questions during and at the end of presentations is one way of overcoming this problem. Paying attention to nonverbal language may also be a means of picking up possible confusion. What we often see as "strange questions" can also be a tip-off that things are not very clear. Needless to say, a lack of clarity defeats the learning process and at the same time acts as a de-motivator when the lack of clarity is severe or of prolonged duration.

A Power Relations Approach to Adult Learning

The foregoing models or approaches have been primarily influenced by psychology, and the focus is generally on the individual learner. Merriam, Caffarella and Baumgartner(2007) in their chapter "Critical Theory, Postmodern, and Feminist Perspectives," take an approach to adult learning from a power relations framework. They move from a focus on the individual learner to an analysis of the context where learning takes place. "The larger social systems in society, the culture and institutions that shape learning, the structural and historical conditions framing, indeed defining the learning event" (p. 241). They challenge assumptions about the nature of knowledge, what counts as knowledge, where it is located—for example, whether it is located within the individual or in the society—and how it is acquired. If I live in a white middle class society, I will undoubtedly find that what counts as knowledge will be different than if I live in an African American ghetto or a depressed Latino community. In that same connection, if I live in a middle class white community, I am less likely to value as knowledge those things that have been deemed as knowledge by my counterparts from depressed communities. These differing views of what constitutes knowledge have a significant impact on the planning and development of programs and their effects.

It is at the writer's view that we both shape the world and are shaped by it. Thus our knowledge is a product of the society within which we live and is influenced by many facets of that society, including the government, industry, religion, and the media. It appears that we are continuously being created by educational sources that may or may not have a person "up front" facilitating a specific set of facts. We are most likely unaware of the "knowledge" we are acquiring or how we are shaped by it. It becomes then our quest to help adults seriously address the questions of identity that McLaren (1997) poses for us:

Has the social world fashioned me in ways I no longer desire to identify? In what directions do I desire and why? To what extent are my dreams and my desires my own? What will likely be the consequences for me and others both like me and different from me? To what extent is society inventing me and by what moral, epistemological, political, or transcendental authority is this taking place? How am I to judge the world that made me, and on what basis can I unmake myself in order to remake the world? (p. 25)

Lindeman's quote seems a fitting directive at this point when he says that education "begins not with subject matter but with the situations and experiences which mold adult life" (Linderman, 1925, p.33). What we are confronted with in this approach is the concept of critical pedagogy. Brookfield states that "critical pedagogy becomes a means by which students are helped to break out of oppressive ways of thinking and acting that seem habitual but that have been imposed by the dominant culture" (1995, p. 209).

According to Welton,(1995), the aim of critical theory is to "help people to stop being passive victims who collude, at least partly, in their domination by external forces. Critical theory's liberating project is to name the enemies of human freedom and to point to the possibility of freedom's enlargement" (p. 37). The challenge to us as facilitators is whether or not we are willing to help empower people through the acquisition of learning, to analyze the impact of societal influences as to whether they are emancipatory or oppressive, and to decide from the standpoint of an enlightened view what course of action is most appropriate for them. "Empowerment involves people developing capacities to act successfully within the existing system and structures of power, while emancipation concerns critically analyzing, resisting and challenging structures of power" (Inglis,1997, p. 37). While the choice of direction is always with the individual, or should be, we as adult educators have a responsibility to provide them with sufficient information to know that choices exist and to make one from the position of competence.

Finally, I believe that the most important element of all in teaching adults is your own attitude about them, how you see them. For the most part, they are people who are making important contributions, whose collective experience and knowledge is awesome. Individually they may be richer, more broadly traveled, more socially astute, better known, and more respected in their own right than we who stand before them. In short, they are to be respected. I do not mean to say that if you happen to be the top dog in the room that you should respect them less. I am simply trying to make sure that you are not afflicted with the disease that affects so many in the teaching profession that leads them to hold such condescending attitudes about those they teach.

II
PERFORMANCE NEEDS ASSESSMENT

In order to determine what performance needs exist for which training is needed, some insight into needs assessment/analysis is needed. This skill is important in determining our specific needs. Needs assessments are not generally an area that most persons find alluring. Most are extremely poor at doing them. Irrespective of the foregoing, the needs assessment is the most critical element of the total training design process. Without a proper assessment we will never be able to know what the true needs are. Thus, any objectives we set and any activities we construct to achieve those objectives are based on sand.

Self-Preparation

As we begin the assessment process, the question arises as to who should be assessed first. There are some very good reasons to answer this question by looking into a mirror. Self-assessment is indeed in order. Are we really prepared to meet the client? What do we know about the client, "the person?" What do we know about the business or organization we are proposing to help? What do we know about the industry in general? How knowledgeable are we about our entry skills? What is our philosophy regarding the profession we have chosen? How do we really see ourselves?

How we see ourselves makes a great deal of difference in how successful we will be with our clients and in the profession in general. We need to see ourselves as "business people who specialize in human performance rather than finance, marketing, or operations" (Robinson & Robinson, 1995, p. 12). As such it is reasonable to conclude that we must understand the business or other organizational institution we seek to serve. At the very least, it would appear that Robinson and Robinson are correct when they insist that practitioners in the field should be able to:

- Read the annual report of their organization and *understand* it.
- Discuss knowledgeably with managers and others the ratios used to measure the operational health of the organization in order to compare the current performance of the organization against its goals . . .
- Identify the primary forces, outside the control of the organization that will challenge the organization's ability to discuss the strategies and actions being taken by competitors and the implications of those actions for the organization.
- Skillfully use the business terminology of the organization. (p. 12)

These authors suggest a number of ways we may improve and maintain our competencies in these areas; for example, by reading trade journals and magazines, professional journals, newspapers, reviewing organizational documents, volunteering in situations where relevant information and experience may be gained, and so on. It is important to read outside your regular reading routine. Suffice it to say that continuous knowledge and skill improvement is the order of the day.

Bellman (1992), by way of implication, offers another aspect of our self-assessment and preparation to work with clients. He points out that we must develop a mindset that allows us to work comfortably and effectively, to operate with ease in an environment where we are *not in charge*. He asserts that we have more expertise than authority and that while we do not have the final say, we do have important influence. Our task in this regard is to be able to accurately assess the level and nature of that influence and be prepared to use it strategically. Thus our preparation for working with our clients includes the identification and strategic use of this influence, which if done properly should yield rich results.

The entry phase of the consultation, which precedes and often accompanies the needs assessment activity, requires a well-planned approach supported by solid research and strategic preparation to enhance the probability that we will be able to successfully move through this phase. This forms the basis for the construction of a contract to perform the service indicated by the results of the assessment. A major part of this is self-preparation. We need to be as diligent in this regard as we are zealous in our pursuit of money for work we have completed.

Assessing the Client's Needs

Robinson and Robinson (1995) describe four kinds of needs: business needs, performance needs, training needs, and work environment needs:

> *Business needs* are the goals for a unit, department, or organization . . . *Performance needs* are those on-the-job behavioral requirements of people who are performing a specific job. *Training needs* identify what people must learn if they are to perform successfully. *Work environment needs* identify what systems and processes within the work environment of the performer must be modified if the performance needs are to be achieved. (p. 24)

As we examine the conditions in the workplace, it is vital that we understand how these different needs should be catalogued and dealt with in the overall assessment of the client's needs. Of particular significance is which of these needs can and cannot be resolved through training.

"There are two major methods for training needs assessment: the Problem Analysis Method and the Competency Model Method" (Davis,1974,p.39). He further suggests that all other methods are mere variations of these two types. The Problem Analysis Method, according to Davis, begins with a problem statement and moves through a systematic process to a series of learning needs that are ranked in order of priority. Seven steps are provided in Davis's model:

1. Stating the problem(s)
2. Refining the problem statement
3. Supporting the problem statement
4. Finding the needs
5. Separating learning from non-learning needs
6. Assigning priorities
7. Testing commitment

Problems identified through this method should be handled immediately. They cannot wait to be included in an annual training schedule.

The first step in the Competency Model Method is the development of a competency or behavioral model, which is a specific description of how some task or group of tasks are to be performed. They become the standards by which the performance or knowledge of persons may be measured. There are six steps in this model provided by Davis:

1. Developing a competency model
2. Discovering present levels of performance of each individual by comparing their performance with the competency model
3. Specifying needs (Needs become the deficits between what the model requires and the actual performance of the individual.)
4. Separating learning from non-learning needs
5. Assigning priorities (determining which of the needs are more important)
6. Testing commitment. Determining how committed your client is about carrying out the training. While the concern of how much money the client is willing to spend is important, if that is all the client is willing to do, you may want to rethink your commitment to be involved. You will need a commitment of time and involvement as well as a commitment to accept significant responsibility for the success of the intervention. Block (2011) insists on a 50/50 share of responsibility.

It can easily be seen that this model can be useful in providing organized and sequenced learning for individuals and groups. It is also useful in providing learning for total job competencies. A complete reading of Davis's book is recommended regardless of the fact that it was published a number of years ago.

It may be useful here to define the construction of the term training as used in this book. Training is defined as organized learning experiences over a specified period designed to bring about the possibility of performance improvement on the present job (Nadler & Nadler, 1990). The author of this definition is careful to point out that training may bring about the "possibility" of performance improvement, as no one can say for certain that merely because training has occurred, the learner will use it. There are many factors that may affect whether or not it will be used.

Nadler and Nadler (1990) also differentiate between training, education, and development. Training is for the job or task the person is doing now, education is for those tasks or that job that the person will do soon. Development may not be related to either. These differences are vitally important to the evaluation process. The first two have to be evaluated quite differently, and the third probably need not be evaluated at all except perhaps to determine the impact on staff retention or whether in some general way employees were in a better position to grow with the organization.

Some discussion may be useful regarding those things that give rise to training needs. These needs are often caused by changes in the way work is to be performed. New competencies may need to be mastered. New equipment may also require additional training. Changes in the size or characteristics of the work group could also cause such a need. The behavior, and thus the level of functioning, of groups can be shaped by their size, general composition, the specific proportional representation of various differences among the members, and the characteristics of their members (Harrison, 1987). For example, "when women or members of an ethnic group are in the minority in management . . . they may feel pressures to overachieve or to minimize their visibility (Kanter, 1977). These pressures and resulting behaviors may well affect interpersonal and/ or intergroup performance. "Divergences in social background, work experience, and professional training can also lead to conflicts about how work should be conducted and about values and goals" (Harrison, p. 55). Inter-minority and dominant minority conflict is likely to arise in multicultural settings and give further rise to training needs (Welch, 1995). These conflicts generally arise from goal incompatibilities between, and sometimes among, groups. New products, programs, geographic areas served, clientele, and the presence of a new supervisor may also become a cause for training needs.

Over the last several years, we have come to more readily accept that a multicultural work force gives rise to additional training and education needs. Training to assist persons in acculturating, training across cultures to improve their abilities individually and collectively, in working together, as well as additional training for leaders who must lead and manage these populations is being recognized as a necessity. All of these changes and more give rise to training needs.

While it is obvious to most that significant change will more likely than not result in increased training needs, some changes are made in small increments, so small that they are not immediately noticed. They, by themselves, may not require any action. However, over time they may accumulate and cause a significant reduction in staff competence. Because these changes and additions may be slight and unnoticed over the period, we often think that the staff has *lost* competence when instead they have never had it when it comes to doing the job task as it has come to be configured. We must therefore keep careful notice of all changes and review them routinely to determine the extent to which they may have impact upon the competency levels of the staff as well as those who lead them.

Often changes we call for or those imposed from externals or above may affect our competencies. They may affect our ability to do the various tasks we are responsible for, or they may affect our ability to manage the personnel doing the task. It would behoove us to assess this probability prior to making the change and, should the effect warrant it, plan for the training along with planning for the change.

There are three types of training needs as relates to the domains of learning: cognitive, psychomotor, and affective:

1. Cognitive training needs are those needs that involve knowledge, information.
2. Psychomotor needs are those needs that involve the skill to do something.
3. Affective needs have to do with those attitudes, feelings, values, and beliefs that will be most helpful in doing something (or not doing something).

In order that all types of needs are identified, we must deliberately search for them in the assessment. For example:

> **Problem**: People don't answer the telephone correctly, and it's affecting customer sales.
> **Need**: To have people answer the telephone correctly and improve customer sales.

Before we can proceed to correct this problem or fill this need, we must first get a more specific description of just what the problem is. For example, what is it persons are doing that causes you to conclude that they are not answering correctly? You can proceed by asking for specific examples, or you can establish a competency model. This would be a statement or series of statements describing very specifically the correct way to answer the telephone. Once we have this model, we can assess the degree that the person's competencies match the model.

We must bear in mind, however, that merely because there is a discrepancy between what should be done and what is done or between how something is done and how it should be done, this does not in itself constitute a training need.

Before we assign it for training, it must be established that the discrepancy is not due to some factor other than a training need. For example, is there some structural problem that interferes with the person's ability or willingness to "answer the phone properly"? An example could be that the location of the telephone and other job requirements interfere.

Often the problem is that the employee has so many tasks to perform in the time allotted that proper performance is impossible. No amount of training can remedy this problem. If it is a training problem, it is certainly not one for the employee; rather it is one for the employee's supervisor. One to assist him or her in recognizing who or what the culprit really is and correcting his or her own supervisory performance.

It is important to note early that wherever possible we must gain as much information as needed from a variety of sources. In the current example, the direct supervisor of the telephone operators and persons who are recipients of their service would be a good start.

There is always the possibility that the employee is not aware of the discrepancy. This is the case probably more often than we recognize. Has anyone told them specifically, or at all, that they are not answering correctly? Do they answer the telephone often? In those areas, where our performance is occasional, it may understandably be deficient. As can be easily surmised by the foregoing questions, what may be needed is merely feedback or practice (or both). Training would, in such cases, not only be unneeded but quite possibly be counterproductive.

Every discrepancy that can be corrected by training need not be dealt with. One of the questions to ask is does it really matter? If we did nothing, what real difference would it make? What impact would its resolution have on the organization's or the group's effectiveness? If the answer is that the resolution of the discrepancy would have little positive effect, it may be well to go on to more significant discrepancies. The focus of the HRD practitioner on performance as it relates to the achievement of the organization's goals cannot be overstated. Robinson and Robinson (1995) make the point quite powerfully:

> For too long the HRD or training professional has focused on the *activity* of training; people in the profession thought of themselves as specialists associated with some aspect of learning, such as designing the courses, delivering the programs, or identifying the needs. That focus will no longer suffice in today's business environment. We must shift from focusing on what people need to learn (training) to what they must do (performance). (p. 7)

In any discussion about needs determination, it must be emphasized, as stated above, that it is important, vitally so, to begin with an identification of the organization's needs. Individuals may have a myriad of needs, which may be satisfied without any positive effects on the organization whatsoever. Therefore, it would be a waste of the organization's resources to concentrate on such needs unless they are authorized by the organization under their "development" needs as defined by Nadler and Nadler (1990). In the case of development, the objective would not be an improvement of performance on the job, although there may be some serendipitous effect in some instances.

Once it has been decided that the discrepancy is in fact a training need, that it is a performance discrepancy that can be resolved through training, we then examine the difference between what the competency model calls for and the actual performance. To the extent that they do not match, that extent would represent the training need or needs. We would then have to ask, regarding the task the person needs to perform:

- What knowledge does the person need to have to perform this task?
- What skill does the person or persons need to have to perform it?

◘ Finally, what attitudes, feelings, values, and/or beliefs would be most helpful? Most hindering?

From these questions you will have generated a list of training needs in the three domains: cognitive, psychomotor, and affective. A participatory illustration may be useful, one that I begin, and you, the reader, make additions to:

Cognitive
What information do they need to answer the telephone correctly?

◘ Specific required wording (what should the person say when answering?)
◘ Number of rings permissible before answering
◘ How to handle angry customers
◘ In specific terms, what additional information they are to give to the caller

Psychomotor
What skills do they need to do this?

◘ Be able to speak with appropriate verbal, nonverbal, and paraverbal skills. (These would have to be specifically spelled out so that their meaning is clear to the learner.)
◘ Be able to defuse, manage, or resolve conflict over the telephone.

Affective
What attitudes, beliefs, values, and feelings would be most helpful? Hindering?

◘ That calls are not "interruptions"
◘ That customer service is in their best interest too
◘ That the angry caller's display is not personally directed at them
◘ "I value self-control."

Don't forget to make your extended list. The one above, as you can see, is by no means exhaustive.

19

Methods and Techniques of Needs Assessment

A brief overview of some of the methods and techniques of needs assessment is in order. The reader is encouraged to research more detailed descriptions of those of interest as well as explore many that are not listed here. The following list represents those to be covered in this section:

- Observation
- Individual interviews
- Group interviews
- Randomly selected group interviews
- Questionnaires and survey instruments
- Critical incident method
- Behavioral scales
- Force field analysis
- In-basket exercise
- Assessment centers
- Task Analysis

Observation

Observation has long been a method of analyzing or assessing the performance of individuals and groups. It has its advantages and its drawbacks as well. If it is done with the performer's knowledge, it may cause the performer to behave differently than he or she would ordinarily; thus the observer would be precluded from what we might term an actual or authentic performance. When the observation is being done unobtrusively, the behavior may be authentic, but we are sometimes unable to understand the context in which it is occurring and therefore draw appropriate conclusions.

Individual interviews

Individual interviews are one of the most common ways in which needs are assessed. Perceptions are sought from interviewees as to what the problems or needs are. This method is also used to determine what questions should be used on surveys or what areas should be considered for in-depth consideration.

One of the major problems with interviews is not so much the method itself as it is the poor planning of the interview questions and process by the interviewer. This may also be said of the interviewing techniques. Many people lack the skills required for an effective interview. For example, the results of the interview may be rendered useless by behaviors of the interviewer that have the effect of biasing the responses of the interviewee. They may not understand the importance of eliminating, to the extent possible, semantic, mechanical, and psychological barriers that may be prejudicial to the outcomes of the interview.

Group interviews

Group interviews are effective methods of gaining insights regarding the needs of not only the individual members themselves but also larger units within the organization. It can yield critical data on interrelationships. This is of great importance to management in that it is not so much the individuals on which we focus as we seek to manage; rather it is the relationships between them. There are a variety of methods available to use in group interviews; for example, from brainstorming to simulations. A well-stocked repertoire of such activities is highly recommended.

Randomly selected group interviews

This method is often convenient and appropriate in cases where there are a large group of persons involved, where it would not be feasible to interview each member, and where discrete units would not suffice. When such methods are used and the sample size is sufficient, the responses or results from such groups can often be generalized to the larger population from which they were taken.

Questionnaires and survey instruments

Questionnaires and surveys can be used in almost any situation. However, they are particularly useful when attempting to cover large numbers or geographical areas. Persons planning to use this medium are encouraged to spend a great deal of time researching the development, administration, and interpretation of the results of these instruments. It may be well to note that in many cases the organization as well as the respondents may have some trepidation about the use of these instruments, although for different reasons. Both will most probably have concerns about what will happen to the information, who will see it, how they will be affected by it, and so on. These concerns must be dealt with early on.

One caveat about overreliance on instruments for needs assessment is given by Dixon (1990): "Instruments only cover stated needs. To get at real needs, HRD practitioners must communicate extensively with the customer" (p. 13).

The critical incident method

This method generally uses no more than three questions, which are stated in both positive and negative terms. For example, describe a way that you heard a particular person answer the phone that you feel was superior. This could be stated or asked negatively. For example, describe the way you heard someone answer the telephone that you would consider unsatisfactory. You could ask them to repeat what and how a person answered as opposed to describing the way they answered.

Supervisors often use the critical incident method in determining why they feel a person or a group of persons have performance discrepancies. They are asked to list those incidents that occur over a specified period that lend support to their conclusion that training is needed. Care must be taken to assure that the information is accurate as sometimes individual's reflect descriptions they feel serves them best.

Behavioral scales

Behavioral scales are a descriptive list of specific behaviors that are required of a particular group or class of employees. The scales are listed with the top items rated highest to the lowest at the bottom. One such scale in reasonably wide use is the Behaviorally Anchored Rating Scale. The scales have been used to identify the highest and best use of the training effort. Priority for training would run from top to bottom.

Force field analysis

Kurt Lewin's force field analysis method is one of the more familiar techniques utilized in a variety of fields yet often overlooked as a viable tool for use in the assessment of needs. It is like the seesaw most of us played on as children. For every force that moves in one direction there is a counterforce moving in the other. Thus, using the force field approach we would ask what the driving forces are that would cause one to answer the telephone correctly. What are the opposing or restraining forces that would cause the person not to do so? If the force that restrains the person from answering the telephone correctly is stronger than the force that moves the person toward correct behavior, then the person will most likely not answer correctly. If we can identify the forces at work, we can either strengthen one or reduce the strength of the other, either of which should serve our purpose, that of having the person answer correctly. The scenario could be stated another way. We could ask what forces drive the person to answer the telephone incorrectly and what restraining forces militate against such behavior. The process would be the same.

Brainstorming, round robin, nominal group technique, and slip writing are a few of the many techniques that may be used to identify driving and restraining forces. These may be used with a variety of group sizes. The Delphi technique is one, among others, that will serve well where subjects are scattered over a wide geographical area. With today's level of technology individuals over widely dispersed locations can easily be accessed.

The in-basket exercise

The in-basket exercise is a simulation of an actual situation where the in-basket contains several items that may be modified to fit the conditions under which the person or persons being assessed would be expected to perform. They would be rated on how they performed. Analysis is made of their performance establishing the basis for the training needs analysis. Time limits may be adjusted to increase or decrease the intensity of the exercise.

Assessment centers

Assessment centers may be used to provide a realistic setting as near to the actual work situation as possible. This, it is argued, provides the closest thing to authenticity possible outside the actual work setting and therefore is fairest to the persons being assessed. Candidates are generally grouped and required to participate in activities while trained observers record their behaviors. The average assessment period is from three to five days. A thirty-year follow-up study by Anstey (1978) is revealing. The proportion of persons who rose to high-level positions varied directly with their scores in the assessment process (Keil, 1981).

Task analysis

Task analysis is defined by Michalak and Yager as "a method for specifying in precise detail and in measurable terms the human performance required to achieve a specific management objective, the tools and condition needed to perform the job, and the skill and knowledge required of the employee" (1979, p. 43). Noe (2010) defines it as a method that "identifies the important task and knowledge, skills, and behaviors that need to be emphasized in training for employees to complete their tasks" (p. 103).

In performing a task analysis, the job is divided into parts and the performance for each part is described so that performance can be measured and needed training may be decided in advance. Additionally, deficiencies in performance of those presently holding the job may be identified and appropriate training provided. A thorough task analysis really determines the training curriculum for us.

These are but a few of a long list of methods available to the practitioner. The list should provide strong reinforcement for the importance of the human resource development practitioner toward the development of an in-depth knowledge and a high degree of skill in a variety of assessment methods. Assessment forms the very foundation of the training effort. Without a firm foundation, subsequent training efforts will not provide the possibility of improved job performance (Nadler & Nadler, 1994).

Having examined various methods, there are still other considerations. For example, Pike (1989) insisted that in order to be sure that you have the correct set of needs, it will be necessary to use "non-repetitive redundant measures. This means we must assess the needs in at least two different ways" (p. 8). He goes on to explain that "non-repetitive redundant measures provide two different methods for looking at the same information. Non-repetitive means that the measure does not repeat itself. Redundant refers to the fact that it measures the same thing" (Pike, 1989, p. 9). For example, observation of a target group may give you information about a given task. However, when their customers are interviewed, you may well find a different slant. You have used two different measures to assess the same thing. The results are that you have a more complete and accurate picture of the actual need.

It is also useful to note that consideration must be given to three groups of people: the senders, the sendees, and the payers (Pike). You will need the support of those who are sending the trainees, most likely the supervisors or managers of the department in which the sendees work, as well as those who must pay for it, the people who are responsible for the budget, and they are *not* always the same. If you wish repeat business or referrals from them (or both), their wants and needs must be considered in the very beginning. Pike also insists that we:

Get input from one level up and one level down when doing any needs assessment. For example, if you're designing training for supervisors, ask both the supervisors' managers for input and the supervisors' employees for input as well. The training target group may not clearly see its own needs. (1989, p. 8)

One tool in use is the 360 degree feedback model described in issue number 9508 of Info-Line of the American Society for Training and Development as "a questionnaire that asks people—superiors, direct reports, peers, and internal and external customers—how well a manager performs in any number of behavioral areas." Organizations themselves generally establish 360 degree systems. For an internal practitioner this would be an excellent source for performance needs. A practitioner external to the organization could easily adapt the bare technique of the complete circle of inquiries in such a system to meet assessment purposes.

We can easily see the efficacy of this approach. We can as easily see that we must be alert to the need for helping some clients develop a higher appreciation for and an understanding of the needs assessment process or they are likely to balk at the time it often takes and its seeming obtrusiveness. You can also well imagine the resistance that many supervisors may have when they find that their subordinates are evaluating them. Many have never had that experience and may be fearful of it.

The HRD practitioner must also be able to distinguish between the offerings of the subordinates as to which is truly substantive and which may be motivated by factors outside the interest of the further development of either the supervisor or the organization. There may be a tendency on the part of some subordinates to "dump" on their supervisors for a variety of reasons. Our job becomes that of separating from their responses that which is useful from that which is not.

The effectiveness of the training function lies in the trainer's ability to solve problems that result in improved performance and an increase in the for-profit organization's bottom line. In the nonprofit organization there would have to be a significant increase in service provided with a decrease in cost that can be directly attributed to the training. It is well settled that the likelihood of this becoming a reality is greatly dependent upon a substantial investment of time in the identification and analysis of performance needs that directly impact the effectiveness of the organization. Whatever approach or combination of approaches selected, if it is appropriate and is skillfully done, the first stage of the process in the designing of training should be off to a very healthy start.

III
PERFORMANCE OBJECTIVES

Now that you have completed your performance needs assessment and separated the performance needs into those than be corrected by training (training needs) from those performance needs requiring a different intervention—for example, an organizational development intervention—you are ready for the next step, which is constructing performance objectives to satisfy the training needs.

The question is often asked why so much emphasis is placed on objectives. Why are they so important? Principally because they form the basis of virtually everything else you will have to do. They tell you the content of the session, provide insight as to the methods you may have to apply, and provide a concrete basis for measuring whether or to what extent the outcomes have been achieved. Equally important is the fact that well-written objectives provide learners with a clear statement in advance of what they must learn and/or how well they must perform in order to be successful in the learning experience. This is consistent with the basic tenets of adult learning theory.

Terminal Objectives

You will need to construct *terminal objectives*. Terminal objectives represent the end results, what you want people to know, do, or believe at the end of training. For example, your objective may be to become competent in designing training experiences. Let's accept that as the terminal intent. At the end of the training session or sessions we would expect you to be able to perform all of the competencies necessary in the design of training. If you wished to become a competent trainer, it would require more than design skills. Thus you would have to have more than one terminal objective; for example, one for the design portion and one for the behavioral portion of the required competencies. If you think of a pilot, you can see readily that he or she would need to be competent in several major areas and thus require terminal objectives in each of these areas, such as navigation, aeronautics, armaments, and so on. Football players must not only become competent in the physical elements of the sport but must master the playbook as well; two very different competencies. In general, terminal objectives are appropriate for each major competency to be learned.

Enabling Objectives

Enabling objectives represent all of the things you would need to know or do and/or feel or believe in order to reach terminal competency. In the example given above regarding becoming a competent designer of training, should we accept that as the terminal objective, we would address the question what would you need to learn in order to be competent in training design? To name a few things, we can start with learning assessment, constructing performance objectives, selecting learning activities, and selecting learning strategies. These would represent enabling objectives, the objectives that would enable the learner to reach the level that he or she could become competent in the design of training.

Requirements of a Performance Objective

The requirements of a performance objective, whether it is a terminal or an enabling one, are the same. They must state the performance in measurable terms, state the criteria, standard, or the level of acceptable performance (all mean the same), the conditions under which the learners must demonstrate that that they have mastered the intent of the objective, and how or by whom will the foregoing be confirmed. Let's take them one by one.

Performance

The performance is the "what" of the objective. What do you want the person to know, do, or feel? The performance must be stated in measurable terms. What can be observed in some form that lets one know that the learners know what was intended for them to know, can do what was intended, or feel, value, or believe what was intended? If this cannot be observed in some measurable way, we do not have the first required element of a performance objective.

It is important to keep in mind the importance of the words used to illustrate the measurability element. These words themselves must be specific. To "know" is not specific, as it still leaves the question of how we will determine when the learner really knows. If, for example, we ask the learner to list something, we are then able to determine that he or she knows. Thus, such phrases as the following can be considered as specific and would be used in behavioral objectives:

To state	To write
To list	To solve
To identify	To gather
To compare	To name
To explain	To role-play
To assemble	To contrast
To match	To solve

The following list of phrases are often used but should not be used in behavioral objectives without behavior indicators (discussed later), as they are general in nature:

To know
To understand
To fully understand
To believe
To appreciate

These lists are not exhaustive but are merely examples. A word that often appears in objectives is "correctly." Correctly is not sufficiently specific to be used alone. It leaves us with the need to determine what correctly really means. We must therefore find ways to determine what a person would have to know in order to demonstrate that they know how to answer "correctly." We would then have to decide how we wished to have the learner demonstrate that knowledge to us. If the learner is, for example, able to list or write the steps and words to answering the telephone as required by the criteria established for answering, we can safely assume that he or she knows how to answer the telephone correctly.

Criteria (standards or level of acceptable performance)

The second requirement of a performance objective is the criteria, standard, or level of acceptable performance: how well must the learner perform; what quality of performance is required, and so on. As an example, let's say that the performance we wish is that the learners will be able to construct a performance objective, and the learners submit the following:

> Given four hours of instruction on constructing performance objectives, participants will be able to write a performance objective.

The objective has the performance stated in such a manner that it is indeed measurable, and thus the first requirement of a performance objective is clearly met. The second requirement is clearly not met; there is no criteria stated as to the quality of the performance expected of the learners. We have learned at this point that we must state how well the performer must perform in order for the performance to be acceptable. So let's try again:

> Given four hours of instruction on constructing performance objectives, learners will be able to write a performance objective that includes all of the requirements given during the session.

Although it is acceptable in that it does state the criteria, we could have made it more specific by spelling out the requirements so that there would be no doubt in the mind of learner or the facilitator of learning:

> Given four hours of instruction on constructing performance objectives, learners will be able to write a performance objective that states the performance in measurable terms, the criteria, conditions, and how and/ or by whom the requirements criteria will be confirmed.

The learner can easily see and understand clearly what is expected of him or her and therefore is in better position to achieve the outcome should they desire to do so. It is also clear to the instructor what has to be presented as well as how; what materials, strategies, and other learning paraphernalia would be necessary to facilitate the learning the objective requires.

There are many ways to establish criteria. Learners can be asked to perform, for example, according to some standard in an industry, to some code, in accordance with certain legal principals or precedents. Students are often required to write papers in accordance with the current edition of the publication manual of the American Psychological Association. If this is established as one of the bases on which the quality of the paper is to be judged, then it would be considered a criteria.

Conditions

The third requirement of a performance objective we must consider is the condition we attached to the performance objective. What are the givens, the permissions, or the restrictions under which the learner must demonstrate terminal competency? For example:

> Given a drawing desk, drafting paper, a T-square, an architect's scale, and a triangle, students will complete a floor plan to scale 1 = 20 from written descriptions given by the instructor.

Here we are focusing on what is given, which is a restriction actually in that the student would be expected to complete the assignment with only those items listed in the objective. So we have learned that restrictions and givens are all conditions.

Conditions or restrictions should be related to workplace performance expectations. If a receptionist, for example, is expected to operate the phone system in a very busy, stressful, and noisy environment, you would want to create a condition that is quite similar and establish that as the condition under which the person must answer.

> Given a three-hour learning session on telephone etiquette, participants will be able to answer the phone without assistance in an instructor-prepared simulation in accordance with the criteria established in the session.

"Without assistance" then becomes the "condition" under which the person must perform. If he or she answers the phone, in accordance with the criteria given and without assistance, the person has "passed."

Confirmation

The fourth requirement of a performance objective is confirmation. By what means will the confirmation be effectuated? We have stated what we want people to do, learn, or feel, we have set the standards requirements, and we have established the conditions, but how do we know that all of this has happened? Someone(s) or something must verify and sometimes judge that the performance happened according to the requirements that have been set. At the end of training it could be the facilitator, in the classroom the teacher, or it could be a computer printout, and so on. The point is that there has to be verification that the task has been performed and the standards met under the established conditions.

For an illustration, let's go back to our earlier performance objective concerning participants being instructed on writing performance objectives:

Given four hours of instruction on constructing performance objectives, learners will be able to write a performance objective that states the performance in measurable terms, the criteria, conditions, and how and/ or by whom the completion of the requirements will be confirmed without reference to notes or other assistance. The facilitator will determine whether the criteria have been met.

It is important to remember that it may require several enabling objectives to achieve a single terminal objective. It is also important to note in advance that you may have more than one terminal objective for a session.

Learning Domains

Just as there are needs in each domain (cognitive, psychomotor, and affective), the objectives to achieve them must be written in the particular domain they represent. Thus, cognitive objectives must be constructed clearly in the cognitive domain just as the psychomotor and affective objectives must be so constructed.

Some review of each domain is in order. The cognitive domain refers to information or knowledge, the psychomotor domain refers to one's ability to do something—a skill—and the affective domain refers to those attitudes, feelings, values, and/or beliefs that may help or hinder a person in learning or applying some knowledge or skill or both. Examples of each are listed below:

Cognitive

Given a three-hour learning experience on answering the telephone, participants will complete a written instructor-devised test with a score of ninety-five out of a possible score of one hundred. Participants may not refer to notes nor confer with one another. The level of acceptable performance will be determined by the facilitator.

Psychomotor

> Given a three-hour learning experience on answering the telephone participants will answer, in accordance with criteria given by the instructor, all of the situations presented in a simulation during the session, without assistance. The level of acceptable performance will be determined by the instructor.

Here again a percentage was given as the standard necessary for approval. The standard was given as 100 percent in that the learner was expected to perform the task correctly in "all" situations presented. Percentages are not always used, nor are they appropriate in all situations.

It is also useful to note that a person can "know" how to do something without being able to actually "do" it. That is to say that I may have the information in my head as to the correct way to answer the telephone but may not be able to actually answer it correctly. The former speaks to knowledge (the cognitive domain), and the latter speaks to skill (the psychomotor domain).

Each domain will have to be evaluated differently. We can determine whether or not the learner knows the actual words to use in answering the telephone correctly by having the person write or recall them. What we cannot tell from a cognitive perspective—for example, having the person write the correct response—is whether or not he or she can actually utter the words correctly. Nor can we determine whether or not he or she can use the appropriate voice inflections to convey the meaning we intend to have conveyed. We must therefore have the person demonstrate in such a fashion that this is apparent to us.

Affective

> Given a three-hour learning experience on answering the telephone, participants will demonstrate their valuing the methods presented by such unsolicited behaviors as:

- seeking, voluntarily, more information or training opportunities during the session
- planning various uses of the information
- assessing their present levels of knowledge and their present telephone habits
- seeking feedback on their present levels of skill in answering the telephone

And by such unsolicited comments as

- If I had this training before . . .
- This could help me in/when . . .
- I can see now why _____ happened.

The level of acceptable performance will be determined by the instructor.

As can be easily detected in the three examples, the affective objective is significantly different. That is because you cannot *see* or *directly observe* the affective domain as you can those in the other domains. In the cognitive domain the person can demonstrate in ways that are directly observable by the facilitator or instructor except in the cases where the objectives are *covert*. In the cognitive domain, the learner may write, list, state, recall, and so on. In the psychomotor domain the learner may simply perform, acting out the skill either in an actual workplace setting or in a simulated condition. In either case, the facilitator is able to directly observe in some way the indicators that demonstrate learning. Not so in the affective domain. Here we must depend on *secondary indicators of unsolicited comments and behaviors* to indicate to us that the learner has internalized the attitudes, feelings, values, or beliefs that we wanted. *It must also be stressed that a combination of several of these things must happen before we can suggest that such internalization may have occurred.*

It may be well to remind ourselves at this point, as we seek to measure the effectiveness of the session we are building, that we must make this measurement at the end of training, *not* after the learner has returned to the job. That would be an impact evaluation and most probably would be done by the learners' supervisor; as well it should be unless that was a part of your initial agreement or a subsequent amendment. We, therefore, must be looking for indicators that will tell us what we want to know, at least by the final day. The more back-home reality is reflected during the session, the more likely we will see those secondary indicators we are looking for.

Many persons have experienced or certainly been aware of situations where employees were sent to training for specific needs and, after receiving the training, returned to the workplace with little noticeable difference in performance. In many such cases, those responsible for sending persons to training and/or paying for it may have become disillusioned with that particular company, with an individual facilitator, or with training in general. There are times that this may well be the fault of the training, the methodology, or the facilitator (or all of the above).

At least two additional factors need to be taken into consideration. First, that training may well increase the knowledge or skill or even affect attitudes during the session, but it cannot guarantee a change in performance on the job. The evaluation at the end of a session tells us only what the learners know or are able to do at the end of the session. Secondly, there are many things to consider as to why the learners may not be performing on the job after training. Are they given opportunities to use their new or improved knowledge or skill? Without opportunities for their use and without feedback on that use, the knowledge or skill will diminish rapidly. A careful check needs to be made as to any impediments to using the training. It could be structural or something as simple as a supervisor deriding the new information or skill. *It could well be that the learners do not value the learning and do not believe it will be helpful to them.*

The affective domain provides a means by which we are able to focus on developing the kinds of attitudes, feelings, beliefs, and values that will enhance the chances that learners will in fact use what they have learned. When we have developed the knowledge and skills of the learners, we may be only two-thirds done. There are times, situations, where we will find that we have no need to concern ourselves with this area. Learners already have the appropriate attitudes, feelings, etc., to use them, at least in our judgment. Just as often, however, we will find the opposite.

In any discussion about objectives, in the affective domain in particular, some reference must be made to Krathwohl, Bloom, and Masia (1964), whose publication has formed the foundation for subsequent laborers in this area. These authors provide us with five levels of learning in the affective domain. The extent to which we wish the learners to be "affected" becomes the primary guide to what we do in the way of activities as well as how we allocate time allotted for the achievement of the levels we seek. The context in which the training occurs will also be a determinant as to whether or not achieving the desired level is realistic.

The five levels provided by Krathwohl, Bloom, and Masia (1964) are:

1.0 Receiving (Attending) [which includes] awareness
2.0 Responding [which includes] acquiescence in responding, willingness to respond,
3.0 Valuing [which includes] acceptance of a value, preference of a value, [and] commitment . . .
4.0 Organization [which includes] conceptualization of a value, [and] organization of a value system.
5.0 Characterization by a value or value complex (pp. 176-184)

As can easily be seen by the five levels presented by Krathwohl, Bloom, and Masia (1964), the task of the HRD practitioner is indeed a considerable one when it comes to the oft-repeated request of clients to "change the attitudes" of their employees and more often than not to do so in three hours or less. This is particularly true when it comes to issues of diversity and multiculturalism. How long it takes to affect the underlying basis of "attitudes" depends among other things, on how deeply the underlying causes have been held as well as for how long. Additionally, the context in which the change attempt is being made is also a vital factor. It may well be that it is not reasonable that such a change can be made by training alone.

Cole (1996) would insist that those prejudices, for example, that are developed early (unintentional prejudices) are more conducive to change through training methodologies than such prejudices that are developed in later life (intentional prejudices). In fact, he insists that the latter are unlikely to be changed by training but that they can best be controlled by authority—power figures such as supervisors insisting on compliance with appropriate rules of conduct. Suffice it to say that careful attention must be paid to the affective area of the design so that the possibility of learners valuing the new information or skill presented is enhanced along with their desire to use it back at the work site.

Let us review the steps in the objective setting process:

1. ***Develop Measurable Terminal Objectives.*** These objectives describe in measurable terms the outcome expected at the end of training; thus the name terminal.

2. ***Develop Measurable Enabling Objectives.*** These are the "sub-objectives" necessary for participants to learn in order to reach terminal competency. In order for a person to be able to "answer the telephone correctly" (terminal objective), what do they have to know? All of those things they need to know that they do not already know constitute potential enabling objectives. Stated another way, *the sum total of the enabling objectives equals the terminal objective they are constructed to achieve*

3. ***Decide the Criteria or Standard.*** Now that you know what you want the learners to know or do, you and the learners will need to know how well they will have to learn or do what is asked for in order for their performance to be considered acceptable. The learner needs to know how good a job he or she must do in order for you to be satisfied so that he or she can determine what effort has to be expended to meet the criteria. The facilitator needs to know the same so that he or she also knows when the learner has achieved the appropriate level.

To illustrate the foregoing, if the objective was that learners would be able to copy a handwritten business letter using a word-processing program on a personal computer, and the learners did copy the letter, this would be measurable and observable. But if it took them one full workday to do the three-quarter page letter, you would probably not be satisfied. You would therefore add a time limit. The same situation would exist if the letter was filled with mistakes. You would want to set a standard for such things. The standard then becomes the level of acceptable performance.

4. ***Decide under What Conditions or Restrictions the Learners Must Perform.*** In the example concerning answering the telephone, you would certainly not be satisfied if the learners kept a colleague with them to coach them while they were in the process of constructing the letter. The objective was to have them reach the level of competency to perform this activity by themselves. Therefore, the restriction imposed was "without assistance."

Restrictions may be positively or negatively stated. They should bear direct relevance to the conditions or restrictions under which the learner is expected to perform in the workplace. If, for example, the person is expected to perform under noisy conditions or where there are several demands on his/her attention at the same time, such conditions should be simulated as closely as possible so that you may be assured that the person will be able to meet the expected performance level required in the workplace.

A simple approach to constructing objectives is to begin with an abbreviated process. Do not try to write the whole objective in the suggested format from scratch. Just ask and answer four simple questions: 1) What do I want them to do? 2) How well do I want them to do it? 3) Under what conditions or restrictions must they show me they know it and can do it? 4) Who will determine or witness that they in fact did it in accordance with the criteria established (who will determine the level of acceptable performance)? The following illustration may be useful:

Measurability element (what do I want them to do?):
Answer the telephone

Level of Standard (how well do I want them to do it?):

◘ In accordance with the criteria given during the session
◘ In all situations presented during a simulation

Conditions under which they must answer the telephone:

◘ Without assistance

Who will determine the level of acceptable performance (who will determine whether they actually answer the telephone in accordance with the established criteria)?

◘ The facilitator

Now that we have the essential elements of the objective we wish to create, it should be a great deal simpler at this point to smooth out the language. Many persons, particularly in the beginning stages, have difficulty dealing with both the specificity of the elements and the language simultaneously. Using this method, you have the option of dealing with one thing at a time. After all, while language is important, the most important thing here is the inclusion of the required elements.

Too much cannot be said about the importance of objectives. First of all, a good assessment starts us on our way. Objectives assure us that we are still sighting down the rifle barrel squarely at the bulls-eye of the target. If these two, the needs and the objectives, are not in true agreement, your learning session is already off on a trip to a disaster. This does not mean that the participants will not learn something or that they will not enjoy it or feel that it was a good session. What it does mean, however, is that they will most probably not have learned what they needed to have learned as indicated by the needs analysis, and for which you accountable. It also means that your client is not likely to be satisfied with your services. Should your client not be satisfied, we can reasonably expect your word-of-mouth advertising to be negative. This will affect your bottom line in a hurry. This is particularly true if you accept Block's (2000) rule of thumb that 85 percent of your business should come from referrals, thus word of mouth. It is your clients that sustain and grow your business. Therefore the quality of your work in every element of the process, from assessment through evaluation and closure, ought to reflect this recognition.

IV

ACTIVITIES TO ACHIEVE THE PERFORMANCE OBJECTIVES

Now that the objectives are properly constructed, we arrive at the tasks that all too many practitioners and would-be practitioners rush to begin, namely, the construction of activities to achieve the learning objectives. Many often come to this point with poorly done assessments and objectives (if done at all). Sufficient exhortations have already been given in the previous section about such deficient practices, and therefore the writer makes the assumption that you will not be afflicted with any such malady at this point. Given this assumption, no further exhortations or warnings will be given here.

It must be said quickly that *the activities to achieve the performance objectives must be principally congruent in domain with the objectives they are to achieve.* To illustrate the point; if you wanted to teach a person to *perform* a line dance (skill), it would be exceedingly difficult to do so by simply providing that person with exhortations about the level of popularity he or she would achieve if they became proficient at line dancing (affective approach). This is not to say that such would not serve to possibly motivate the person to learn the skill; however, absent any other input, learning the dance is not very likely. Additionally, the person may already be motivated to learn the dance, thus creating overkill and maybe "turn-off." It is probably obvious to the reader at this juncture that it may take several activities to achieve the learning demanded by a single objective. It is also true that it may not. Additionally, it is useful to note that it may require activities in more than one domain to achieve the proficiency you seek. For example, you may have to give the learner information on how to answer the telephone (cognitive) in order for that learner to master the skill-practice (psychomotor) necessary to answer the telephone. Let's say for the sake of argument that the learner has demonstrated that he or she is able to perform the task as a result of the training you have provided. A question now remains: what are the probabilities that the learner will use this skill (answer the telephone correctly) when he or she returns to the work setting?

The fact that a person *can* do something does not mean that they *will*. The best chance we have of being sure that a person will voluntarily apply their learning after the session is over is that for some reason "*they want to.*" The best reason for learners to want to is that they value it in some way that they believe in it. Succinctly stated, if they have a positive attitude toward the use of the information, it is more likely that it will be used. Thus, it can readily be seen that sometimes not only will more than one activity be needed to achieve a particular objective, but activities from more than one domain may be necessary as well.

Learning activities should be selected or designed with several factors in mind, among them the opportunity for multiple learning and maximum participation of the learner; the experience, education, and training of the learner; the culture of the learner; and the age and values of the learner. Further, the variety of the activities and their sequencing are major considerations as well. The order in which learning activities are arranged can either facilitate or retard learning.

The learning facilitator must have an excellent grasp of adult education theory. It is basic to the training effort. Too often facilitators simply mirror the behaviors of others they have seen or learning situations in which they have been participants. Just as often, we find "ego needs" driving facilitators to impress rather than inform; to tell rather than explore or develop. Given the varied experiences adult audiences present, telling can be a serious mistake unless you are absolutely certain that they know nothing about what you are about to present. Even so, it is recommended that you tell them with a question. It has been observed that the best facilitation is when the learners say of the experience that they have done it themselves.

Knowles (1984) provides us with his concept of andragogy and pedagogy. In their purest forms they are two extremes. Pedagogy moves from the position that the teacher knows what the student needs to know and therefore proceeds to develop a curriculum and to teach them. Andragogy, on the other hand, posits that adults by their very nature are self-directed or else they are not adults. Knowles refers us to the therapeutic counseling definition of an adult, one that takes full responsibility for their own actions. Taking this definition into the learning milieu, we then must come to the view that adults are and should be responsible for their own learning. Knowles also points out that many adults accept their responsibilities in everyday life but when they come to the learning situation revert to the way they were in earlier school years, probably because of the way they were dealt with in prior learning situations. It may be necessary then to redirect this behavior or at least recognize it so that it may be taken into consideration in developing the training strategy.

The writer would suggest that neither pure andragogy nor pure pedagogy would be advisable most of the time. Further, Knowles is not suggesting that it is an either/or situation. They constitute a continuum, which provides us with a versatile tool with which to approach the learning population. There are times when the facilitator should tell, just as there are times when students would be expected to be self-directed. There are also times when it would be appropriate for them to be at various points along the continuum. Wherever possible and appropriate, we should be seeking to help learners become more self-directed. We must also understand what that requires of the facilitator. Among other things it requires a great deal on the part of his/her design skills as well as facilitation skills. For example, what performances are required? What type of activities would best serve the stated objectives? Recall? Problem solving? Recitation? Case study? Modeling? Simulation?

The Experiential Approach

In order to assist learners in becoming more self-directed and to learn best from various activities, an understanding of the experiential approach is necessary, as it is basic to adult learning. Experiential learning is defined by Noe (2010) as:

> A training method in which participants (1) are presented with conceptual knowledge and theory, (2) take part in a behavioral simulation, (3) analyze the activity, and (4) connect the theory and activity with on-the-job or real life situations. (p. 552)

The experiential process begins with experiencing and progresses to publishing, processing, generalizing, and finally application (Pfeiffer & Ballew, 1988b).

The Experiencing Stage

This stage involves an activity of some kind, doing something. This activity can be contrived by the facilitator in that he or she may have decided upon some technique to spark the activity, such as one involving problem solving, negotiation, self-disclosure, and so on. It is also possible to have a true experience serve as the initiator of the experiential process.

The Publishing Stage

The publishing stage involves the participants sharing their reactions to their experiences gained from the activity or their observations if they were not directly involved in the "doing." Pfeiffer and Ballew (1988b) offer various techniques to aid in this endeavor, among them free discussion, subgroup sharing, recording data, and round robin.

The Processing Stage

The processing stage is next in this experiential cycle: sharing one's reactions is only the first step. An essential and often neglected part of the cycle is the necessary integration of this sharing. The dynamics that emerged in the activity are compared, examined, explored, discussed, and evaluated (processed) with other participants (Pfieffer & Ballew, 1988, p. 85).

Several techniques are offered by the authors to assist in this process, including observation, questionnaires, and discussing questions such as what and how. There are others that may be of help in this crucial stage of the process.

The Generalizing Stage

This stage allows opportunities for participants to glean from the process stage principles that may serve them in future situations or help them make sense out of some present dilemma. This step is extremely helpful in the clarification process. We cannot apply well what we do not fully understand. Nor can we see as useful techniques that leave us with only fuzzy or vague ideas or conclusions. Techniques offered by the authors for this stage include writing statements, individual analysis, and sentence completion. The facilitator would do well to assure that he or she is proficient in the administration of these tasks.

The Applying Stage

The fifth and final stage of this cycle is the applying stage. It is at this juncture that participants may plan and implement their new learning. This application step is one that requires diligence on the part of the learners. The learners must be led to understand that changing their behavior, their ways of interacting with their human environment, is neither easy nor automatic. It can be rewarding if we can manage our way *through* the process of application, for it is a process toward an end that is seldom instantaneously achieved. Therefore some emphasis must be placed on the word *through*.

The authors provide the following recommended techniques: goal setting, contracting, interviewing, sub-grouping, and practice sessions. Facilitators of this final stage must understand the importance of not letting the ball drop here. If such becomes the case, then little may come of an awful lot of human investment.

Criteria for selecting Learning Activities

Perhaps some additional thought should be given as to how and what criteria could be used in selecting a particular technique or method. Fred

Margolis (1971) provided a list in a train the trainer series some years ago that I found helpful:

- ◘ *Facilitator's Comfort, Confidence, and Competence.* The facilitator must be brutally honest with himself/herself in this regard. How comfortable are you really? If you are not comfortable with it you probably won't be very confident either, and vice versa. How competent are you honestly? Have you ever facilitated an experience like this? Similar in level of difficulty/complexity? With a group of this composition? If the answer for you is no on all counts, it does not mean that you should not do it. It does, however, provide you with a clear need to do the work necessary to be able to decide that in fact you can successfully perform the session. It may mean taking on an associate. Or it may well be that you will decide that you really should not be the one to conduct the session. An honest answer to the question will at least move you toward the correct decision.

- ◘ *Learners' Comfort, Confidence, Competence.* While it is advisable to "stretch" learners to a point, there is a point beyond which it may backfire. There are situations when some trainees are just not ready to experience nor do they have the background to appreciate in the learning situation. To forge full speed ahead can be disastrous for all concerned. The learners may increase their aversion to training, the facilitator's reputation will certainly suffer, and if the facilitator is attached to a company, so will the reputation and possibly the "bottom line" of the company suffer.

- ◘ *Congruence with Facilitator's Values.* If the training, activities, or any significant part of the experience is not consistent with your values, then you have a decision to make. The writer would suggest that you should probably not do the activity, or the training period, if it is against your values and you cannot get the training or activity changed. You obviously have a philosophy and a set of standards against which you will examine possible engagements. You will have to decide whether these values are seriously held.

◘ ***Congruence with Learners' Values.*** It is vital to the success of the session and your future reputation that you find out as much as you can as quickly as you can about the values of the group. The early part of the session can yield rich data in this regard. If during the needs assessment you are able to gain a great deal of information concerning their values, so much the better. Language and techniques that are inappropriate to them can really upset a group.

◘ You might want to find out just what types of activities and styles they have experienced that they liked and learned well from. You don't have to do the same things, but beware of the risks involved in taking them too far out of their comfort zone. Also consider what subjects are taboos as well. You would not want to run a simulation designed to teach decision making and problem solving that had as its task deciding on who gets a particular organ for a transplant when it is against the religion of the learners to have or condone transplants.

◘ ***Congruence with Desired Objective.*** The activity or activities selected to achieve the objective must be congruent in domain with the objective it is constructed to achieve. That is not to say that there may not be instances where one or more aren't in alignment. Just as in the example given previously, in order to teach a person a skill, they may first have to learn something about it, which may be in the cognitive domain. Suffice it to say that *the sum total of the activities constructed to achieve the desired objective must be* principally *in the domain of that particular objective.* Lectures, for example, are not psychomotor in domain no matter how many times we may use the word skill in the delivery.

◘ ***Maximizing Learner Participation.*** The longer the session proceeds without the learners' active involvement, the farther down the scale of effectiveness the design descends. Learning is enhanced by participation, by experiencing and processing as well as publishing those experiences. Thus learning and participation are difficult to maximize when learners are held suspended over extensive periods by a protracted sermon from the facilitator.

Learners are more likely to internalize experiences that provide a great deal of interaction; very little when they have little or no opportunity to be involved. While most everyone seems to acknowledge this as fact, all too often we find participants sitting through an entire morning without an opportunity to say or do anything.

◘ ***Multiple Learning.*** The highest priority should be given to activities that provide for learning more than one thing. For example, asking participants to keep a diary of their experiences in certain activities can help them to become more proficient at self-examination, learn more about their inter-group reactions and their strategies on given situations, and learn as well how to use this process with others. Another example involves teaching a person to develop a budget while at the same time teaching them to use a particular computer software package.

◘ ***Problem/Performance Oriented vs. Subject Oriented.*** Look for the fitness of the activity to assist participants in solving a problem. For example, your purpose in taking a course in training is not to know more *about* training; rather it is to know how to actually train. Training, says Margolis, is about bringing skills, concepts, and techniques to help others solve their problems. "We work with the trainees problems and so label what we do as 'problem-oriented'" (1971, p. 30).

◘ ***Closeness to Real Life.*** Training that closely approximates the real-life situation of the learner makes internalization of the experience as well as identification with it more likely. The transfer of learning from the session to the workplace is easier for the learner as a result of its closeness to the participant's "real world."

◘ ***Here-and-Now Experiences.*** The facilitator is strongly encouraged to focus on the experiences occurring during the session. Focusing on things outside the learner's experience diminishes the learning possibilities. By focusing on the here and now there is also the added advantage that everyone will be able to join the debriefing of a common experience, thus further enhancing the learning of the total group.

◻ ***Maximize Learner Independence, Autonomy, Feeling of Being Powerful, and Uniqueness.*** The central theme of the facilitator's effort in the learning experience must be the foregoing. One of the basic tenets of adult education is that the learner should, as a result of the deliberate efforts of adult educators, come away from the learning experience with renewed confidence, with a greater sense of autonomy, and certainly "turned-on" to continued learning. If this is kept in mind in the design and implementation stages, if the facilitator's actions are guided by these principles, all will be well.

◻ ***Methodology That Is Most Likely to Achieve the Desired Objective.*** If the design will not in your judgment achieve the objective(s), then no matter how much work you have done to get to this point, there is but one thing to do: throw it out! The author of these criteria tells us that if we haven't thrown out any designs, we need to reexamine our approach, not to mention our concept of quality. It will, for sure, be difficult to trash something you have worked on so hard and for so long. You will rationalize every way possible to avoid it. You probably won't have anyone around to chastise you for the wrong decision, except you. Just remind yourself of what will probably happen if you don't throw it out and the session bombs. That will be a strong motivator to "do the right thing."

◻ ***Artistic Flow.*** You may love lobster, but you probably won't if you eat it every day for a while. The same is true of learning activities. They have to be varied. The facilitator should also be careful, in the sequencing process, not to precede an activity with one that may have a negative impact, and vice versa. The sequencing of the activities of the various modules should be done in such a manner that the achievement of the objectives for that module is assured. Care should also be taken to disperse the types of activities so that participants do not feel overwhelmed by too much of one particular type. A variety of activities, properly sequenced, can be a symphony of learning, an exciting excursion to increased personal and professional competence.

We will probably not be able to have all of these criteria met for each activity or the design at large. They are guidelines for our use as we seek to make our designs the best that they can be for the benefit of those we serve.

Pike (1989) shares another model for consideration in the presentation of training. He has formed the acronym "AIDA" based on the first letters of the names of four major steps into which a presentation or a segment of a training program can be divided: attention, interest, desire, and action.

In the *attention* step, according to Pike (1989), we are often confronted with participants who are preoccupied with their own conversations and/ or concerns that may be internal or external to the training environment. Gaining the attention of the group is an obvious need. One way to do this is by asking a question. If you are running a session on diversity you might ask what challenges participants have encountered or that their division has encountered as a result of diversity. Or what challenges they have observed because their organization has not provided diversity training for its employees. Pike (1989) suggests that the participant responses be recorded on a flip chart and provides three advantages that this technique offers: "1) You break through preoccupation and gain favorable attention, 2) you immediately involve your audience, and 3) the question you ask begins to build a case for why your topic, this particular part of the training program, is important" (p. 20).

In the *interest* step we begin to answer the participant's question "What's in it for me?" It is the question that all participants in every session always ask whether openly or silently. It is a legitimate question, one that not only deserves an answer but also, if an answer is not given, will negatively affect the outcome of the session.

In the *desire* step we begin sharing "the content, the practical how-to's, that we suggested were forthcoming in the attention and interest steps. Here's where we offer the means toward the end results. How can I solve the problem . . . train more creatively" (Pike, 1989, p. 20). We thoroughly explore these kinds of questions in the desire step.

The *action* step is the wrap-up step and "is based on your asking the group, 'What actions are you going to take? What did you learn, and how are you going to put your learning into practice?'"

We have covered some of the critical factors in designing activities to achieve the learning objectives, including how adults learn through the experiential approach, a set of criteria to guide the activity-selection process, and a model for presentation. There are many other critical factors to be considered: facilitator behavior, co-facilitation, and specifics on the use of different methods such as lectures, participatory lectures, case studies, videos, simulations, role-plays, lecture forums, and panels, to mention a few. Suffice it to say that there is an awful lot to know. The focus of this book, however, is primarily on the design phase.

Having said this, let us turn our attention to the construction of the design from which the learning specialist will implement the learning interventions. The term design, as used herein, is often referred to as the facilitator's guide and is in fact the same thing. There is no absolute format for a training design. There are, of course, some things that will always be included. What is presented here is what I have found useful, particularly when teaching persons who are beginning in the field and who wish to be thoroughly prepared. It is an approach that I still use.

First I must share with you a "Welchism," one that serves to establish the criteria for the usefulness of the design as it relates to specificity and completeness. *The design itself should be so specific, so complete in every detail, that another facilitator (assuming that he or she is competent) could conduct the session for which the design was created, achieve the objectives, and do so as well as the designer would have done had he or she been able to be present.* It should be scripted similarly to a play, essentially word for word. The design should include at least the following:

- Terminal Objective(s)
- Enabling Objectives

(Each terminal objective should be listed, and after it each of the enabling objectives needed to accomplish it should be included. If there is more than one terminal objective, each enabling objective or series of enabling objectives necessary to accomplish that particular terminal objective immediately follow it.)

- Activity (ies) to Establish the Learning Atmosphere (often referred to as Climate Setting)
- Activity (ies) to Establish the Learning Contract

- Activities to Achieve Learning Objectives
- Evaluation and Closure Activities
- Materials, Supplies, and Equipment List

All activities are to be time-phased. It is not advisable to use specific time such as 8:30-9:10. Beginning 7 1/2 minutes off schedule in such cases creates unnecessary mathematical computations that may not set well with most persons before the second cup of coffee in the morning. Simply state in the left-hand column how much time is allotted for the exercise. The writer has found it helpful to also include the time allotted in the body of the design, particularly in the instructions to the participants for various task assignments or group exercises.

All theory presentations are attached either inside the body of the design or at the end, and they are complete, word for word. The writer has found it convenient to have loose copies of theory presentations for ease of handling. This is very important when the theory presentation is several pages. Having them in unattached sheets allows you to slide the pages and avoid turning them when reading from a lectern. Turning the pages is distracting, and participants are prone to begin counting pages as opposed to listening. It is hoped that your presentations will be appropriately brief. Number the pages to make it easier to restore them to order and find your place in case you have lost it.

All role-plays are also attached to the design. There should also be a set of instructions for the presenter on how the roles are to be distributed, how to process the experience, and the objectives the role-play is either to achieve or help to achieve.

If there are games to be played or any assignment that require tabulation or calculation, simple straightforward reminders or instructions should be given. Even if you plan to be the presenter, you may well not remember the scoring or calculation procedure that particular day. Or, as aforementioned, you may for some reason not be able to be there; thus someone else less familiar with the items may have to stand in. Always remember that the client comes first. Do whatever is necessary to assure that the scheduled event comes off successfully.

A comprehensive list of all materials, supplies, and equipment must be appended to either the very front of the design or at the end. The site of the proposed session becomes important to you here as what equipment you may need to carry or may have to have in general may depend on what the site is like, what they have, and what cost factors are involved with those things that they can make available to you.

Some of the simplest things can mean disaster for a session because of site problems that you did not properly identify in advance. For example, what about electrical outlets? Not simply are there outlets, but how many and where specifically are they located? Outlets in the wrong place without the ability to be accommodated by extension cords with appropriate floor coverings to avoid people tripping over them can completely alter the configuration of your small-group activities as well as large-group arrangements. Will you need adapters for the outlets? If you are going to use an LCD projector, is there a screen? Is it fixed or portable? Is it of sufficient size? Can it be tilted to maintain viewing quality? Visiting the site, if possible, is well worth the time and effort.

Specificity of language is vitally important most of the time but becomes really important when speaking to someone about a training site or equipment. When you say, "I need five flip charts on stands," what vision do you have? Are you certain it is the same one the person on the other end of the telephone has? Context is important in communication. We develop our context from our experiences and other learning. None of us is exempt from misunderstandings arising from incongruent context. A personal story by the writer illustrates the point. Several years ago, while living in Southern Maryland, I asked a colleague, also a Marylander, living in Baltimore, to join me in conducting a three-day learning experience for a client in Charleston, South Carolina. We agreed, at my suggestion, to meet at one o'clock for a Sunday flight to Charleston with a two-hour-plus stopover in Charlotte, North Carolina. When I arrived at the airport, my colleague could not be found, nor could I reach him by telephone at his home or office. The plane took off with me and a hundred-plus other people but not my colleague. Having waited in the Charlotte airport for two-plus hours, as the flight to Charleston was called, a happy band of persons who had apparently found a better place to wait came to claim their seats on the flight, among them—you guessed it—my colleague. The conversation went something like this.

"I thought you were going to meet me at the airport."

"I did. I was there at one o'clock and obviously so—I caught the plane. Where were you?"

For someone living in Southern Maryland "the airport" means Washington National. For someone living in Baltimore, it's Baltimore

Washington International. We both said "airport." We both visualized "airport." They were certainly not the same. Fortunately for me, my colleague, and especially my client, it all worked out. Context *is* important.

The more specific information you are able to provide and extract, the more likely you and the site representative or intermediary are likely to be communicating accurately. A "large room" is not very specific. "A room 30x40 with solid walls (if privacy is important) as opposed to sliding partitioned walls, with movable chairs, and with temperature controls at our disposal and under our control" begins to get you there.

Suffice it to say that everything that is needed for the session must be listed. "Broad tip" felt markers—how many? What colors? What size masking tape and how many rolls? If you are using video tapes, what are your needs? How many participants are there? Do you need multiple monitors? (You can't have forty people looking at a twenty-one-inch monitor, not to mention four hundred people.) Would a video projector be more appropriate? Will the sound need to be amplified?

The need to be thorough is obvious. One way to amass your list is to go through each module and list everything that's needed. Visualize every activity in the module and list everything you see. Compile your list for all of the modules. Some of the things will be redundant and can be removed at this point.

Some practitioners utilize a checklist for itemizing needs. This may work well for you. If you choose to use this method, make certain that it is sufficiently comprehensive for your purposes. If you decide to construct one, it would probably serve you well to do so by listing all of the things you have used over a protracted period and synthesizing a checklist from your experiences over that period. No matter how satisfactory the checklist appears to be, it will, over time, require revision. Further, close attention is warranted when contracting with unusual clients or situations as you may need things that you ordinarily do not.

Over the past many years of both teaching and training, one request is constant: "Can we see a sample design?" In anticipation of this question from at least some who will read this book, a sample design is presented in Section IX. It is intended to merely show the general format and is not intended as an example to be followed except for that purpose.

In providing training it is useful to remind ourselves that there may be a host of needs we may wish to fill and a tremendous body of information we may be anxious to impart. There is also the fact that there is a limited amount of time when the participants will be available to us. It is therefore necessary to separate what is nice to know from what is essential to know and, given the time available, what is possible to present thoroughly and well.

It is also important to remember that no matter how thoroughly we prepare or how flawlessly we perform, everyone in the session will not come away with every expectation or want fulfilled. We will have to settle for two things: trying to bring about that perfect session one day and understanding, without personal devastation, when it does not happen. It may help to know that we do the best we know at that particular time. If we are true to the position we espouse, what we know will always be changing. Thus, our best performance sails just beyond us, beckoning to us to stay close.

V

FACILITATION

The teacher if he [or she] is
indeed wise does not bid
you to enter the house of
his wisdom but leads you
to the threshold of your
own mind.

Khalil Gibran

The assessment has been completed, the learning program designed, the materials developed and ready, all visuals put in place, and the room arranged, and the participants are ready. Everything is pretty much automatic from here, or is it? No matter how accurate the assessment, how good the design, or how perfectly everything else is attuned to your purpose, if there is a significant deficiency in the knowledge and skills of the person or persons up front, only a miracle will help you avoid sure disaster. There is no overestimating the value of good facilitation skills. While this chapter is by no means exhaustive on the subject, it should not only provide you with valuable insights but also serve as a roadmap to continuous development of the competencies of a skilled facilitator.

Dimensions of Facilitator Effectiveness

Pfeiffer and Ballew (1988a) speak to us about something they term dimensions of facilitator effectiveness. They list them as empathy, acceptance, congruence, and flexibility.

Empathy

Empathy is listed first by Pfeiffer and Ballew, perhaps because of their insistence that "it is crucial that a facilitator try to see things from another's perspective" (p. 9). This, in my view, we must be able to do if we accept the notion that we are to start with participants where they individually and collectively are. It is also necessary to have a good understanding of the other's point of view in order to attend to the needs and wants that are relevant to the learning experience. Without this ability, it would be difficult if not impossible to apply the appropriate attending skills.

Empathy is about feelings. Your ability to sense and respond to them in a positive and effective manner will go a long way in heightening learning and defusing/managing difficult situations that often arise in learning sessions. You will need to stay in touch with your own feelings during the session as well. They will often influence your actions, and that influence may or may not be in the direction that is the most profitable for your session. Your feelings may also serve as a barometer as to what others may be feeling. Whatever the genesis of the feelings you may experience or perceive, remember that all feelings are legitimate. The assumption drawn from a situation that gave rise to the feeling may be incorrect, but the feeling is not. As we move to bring comity in situations where strong feelings are involved, remembering that legitimacy theory may make it easier to remain patient and properly focused.

Karlins and Abelson make the case for our consideration for feelings as a learning tool:

> The creature man is best persuaded
> When heart, not mind, is inundated;
> Affect is what drives the will
> Rationality keeps it still. (1970, p. 35)

Acceptance

Pfeiffer and Ballew (1988a) explain that acceptance is "allowing another person to be different, to have a different set of values and goals, to behave differently" (p. 9). Nothing could be more important, especially during this time in our history, than the ability to be accepting of the diverse values, goals, needs, and beliefs of those for whom we would facilitate learning. Never has it been more important that we value learning from these differences and see them as not just something to be tolerated but to be valued. This is an inner attitude that has to be authentic if we as facilitators would operate at the very peak of our abilities. It also goes to the heart of our ability to be empathetic.

Congruence

"Congruent people are aware of what they are doing and feeling and are able to communicate these to others in a straightforward way. A healthy and psychologically mature person is flexible, not dogmatic, opinionated, rigid, or authoritarian" (Pfeiffer and Ballew, 1988a, p. 9). Self-awareness, self-acceptance, and self-esteem appear to be inextricably interwoven into what Pfeiffer and Ballew term congruence. Knowles, Holton, and Swanson (1988) suggest that we can improve our self-awareness through critical reflection. Critical reflection, says Mezirow (2000), involves a critique of the presuppositions on which our beliefs have been built. This process is one of the preliminary steps toward transformation learning. Critical reflection is not only a self-assessment and self-development tool; it is a method competent facilitators may utilize in helping others toward personal and professional growth.

Learning, in part, according to Mezirow (1990) is a series of revisions of previous experiences. It is a process of reinterpretations, if you will. Many of the assumptions we have and on which we operate in our relations with things and others we have not revisited since we accepted or formed them, especially those we gained in childhood. It is useful, then, to critically reflect on them to determine whether or not we feel the same way about them as we once did, whether or not we wish to keep them as they are, modify them, or get rid of them altogether. Our self-awareness is thus affected by what we decide after a critical analysis of particular assumptions upon which we reflect. Critical reflection, then, is a powerful tool in achieving congruence (Pfeiffer & Ballew, 1988a) and congruence without doubt is an integral part of the skills of a complete facilitator.

Flexibility

The final dimension, flexibility, is posited by Pfeiffer and Ballew (1988a) as an essential ingredient in facilitation. Facilitating learning is about facilitating the possibility of change (Nadler & Nadler, 1994). Change by its very nature is made difficult by the negative characteristics listed by Pfeiffer and Ballew; namely, being dogmatic, opinionated, rigid, and authoritarian. Flexibility is mandated if for no other reason than its being incumbent upon the facilitator to model those behaviors promoted by the learning experience being presented.

Attending

Attending is highlighted by Bertcher (1979) as being among the highly critical skills of the competent facilitator. Lightly defined, attending refers to our ability to show a group or an individual that they have our full attention to what they are saying. "The most important rule of facilitation is to pay attention to the person that is talking" (Rees, 2001, p. 162). This writer has collected a few examples regarding how this can be accomplished:

- Establish good eye contact with the person talking, but do not neglect looking around at the other members of the group as well.
- When you are addressing the group, look directly at each person for several seconds but not in the same sequence in which they are seated. Scan the entire room, looking at the participants randomly. If you have difficulty looking directly into their eyes, look at the center of the forehead just a hair above eye level. If you do it correctly it will appear to them that you are looking directly into their eyes. You can virtually outstare a cat with this technique, so a person should offer no challenge at all.
- Relax, mentally and physically. This will most probably shine through helping group members feel more at ease and thus more inclined toward participating. It will also do wonders for your

ability to think, observe accurately, and do the things required to effectively facilitate.

- Restate what the person has said to you to assure him or her that you are indeed listening. Emphasizing the points that she or he has made also demonstrates that you are listening and will be helpful in clarifying misunderstandings as well.
- Remember that if you pay too much attention to one person it can be problematic. It may cause this person to feel singled out, feel embarrassed, clam up, or do just the opposite—dominate the session. It may also cause others to view you as favoring that particular person and react in ways not beneficial to the purposes of the session.

Movements

Your movements up front should be measured and smooth. Use movement to gain attention, to emphasize, and to establish control when necessary. Move around the group. Moving closer to an individual or group gains attention. Movement can also be a useful technique in getting the more soft-spoken persons to speak louder. By moving away from the person speaking he or she will generally raise their voice to make sure that you can hear them, which will permit their colleagues to hear them as well. Participants most often speak to the facilitator, especially in the beginning of the session. Moving away from the front or where it is difficult for the speaker to see you will also encourage participants to speak to each other.

Gestures

Gestures can be important contributors to the delivery of the spoken word. They can also be a detractor. Needless and exaggerated movements take away from your presentation. They take the listener's attention away from you and place the focus on the movements themselves. What to do with the hands is a big problem for many facilitators. Avoid the "fig-leaf" or six-thirty" position. Don't begin with your hands in your pockets. Later, when you have your audience, and should you choose to slip your hand in your pocket, remember not to move them inside or jingle items that may be inside.

Using questions

Questions are powerful allies in facilitating learning, gaining participation, and in guiding and controlling the flow of dialogue as the need arises. There are several types of questions that many facilitators' use. Some of them are: overhead, direct, open, closed, reverse, relay, imaginative, experiential, and logical. The type of questions to use should obviously be dictated by the objective of the questioner. If a yes or no answer is needed, a closed question would be the appropriate choice.

Closed questions are designed for that purpose, to elicit a yes or no response. Closed questions should be asked when there is only one correct answer. Should the occasion require something other than a yes or no response, when the answer is not known, or when there may be more than one answer, then an *open question* would be the appropriate choice. Often We are not as skillful at phrasing questions as we presume. We sometimes are asking closed questions when the intent was to ask the opposite. What, when, why, how, and so on are good beginning words for open questions.

There are times when we want someone in the group to volunteer to respond to a question or have the entire group focus their attention on the question. In such situations we ask the question of the group. There are times when either we cannot get a volunteer response or we keep getting the same person or persons and the rest of the group remains silent. In these situations a *direct question* would be an appropriate choice. You direct the question to a specific person. Direct questions can be open or closed depending on the type of response the facilitator wishes from the participant.

Situations often arise where sessions become a series of questions from the participants and answers from the facilitator. This is not generally what you would want as a model session. A *relay question* would be helpful here to stimulate thinking and increase participant involvement. In using the relay question, we are asked a question, and instead of answering ourselves, we "relay" it to another person or group of persons. For example, "How would you respond to Rita's question/comment, Loretta?" The relay question can also keep the facilitator from engaging in a confrontation with a participant.

Sometimes facilitators are asked questions to put them on the spot. Other times the facilitator may want the participants to express their own opinion. In these types of situations, a *reverse question* would be the appropriate choice: "Why do you think this may be so, Cindy?"

There are *imaginative questions* that encourage participants to think in new and innovative ways, *experiential questions* that require the participants to use their past experience and past training feelings to respond, and *logical questions* that solicit analytical and sequential thinking.

All of these questions require thought and practice on the part of the facilitator to assure that they elicit the response that the facilitator was seeking.

Silence

Silence on your part can be an asset. Remaining silent long enough to wait out the responses that you are trying to elicit is important. We are often so uncomfortable with silence that we will resume talking before the participant has decided to verbalize their answer to our questions or prodding. That same uncomfortableness leads us to utter such sounds as "um," "ahh," "well," and so on, rather than just pausing and, without looking to the ceiling or the sky for divine inspiration, taking a calm breath, collecting our thoughts, and then addressing the question that has been asked of us.

Facial expressions

Arch Lusberg (1983) insists that our facial expressions are a vital part of our facilitation and our communication with others, whether one-on-one or working with a group. Frowning as if we were weaned on a pickle won't help the participants care very much for us, and we already know that feeling comfortable with the facilitator improves the participants' disposition to learn from us. Smiling inappropriately can be just as troublesome. Expressions should be congruent with the purpose of the dialogue and the situation under which it is occurring.

Facial expressions can also be used to *reward* or to *extinguish* behaviors. Facial expressions that are perceived by participants to indicate approval or disapproval can often cause compliance from the membership. Such signs should be appropriate and carefully thought out. Perhaps the better avenue would be to show approval for appropriate behavior and simply ignore or not reward those things that are not beneficial to the session.

Facial expressions may also work against you. If participants perceive that you approve of what they are saying or doing, they may do more of it if they wish to please you or manipulate you. If they perceive your expression as one of disapproval, they may well stay away from those comments or behaviors not because they wish to change to a more positive stance but merely to deceive. If at that point you are seeking honest open dialogue, it is not likely to occur, as you will have already introduced bias into the situation by your expressions.

Feedback

The ability to give feedback and the ability to truly receive it is an important part of the facilitator's repertoire. It is very difficult to truly assess ourselves. When we elect to ask others for feedback about some facet of our being, we usually ask those whose opinions and feelings most reflect our own, which greatly decreases the likelihood of its accuracy. It may be far better to ask for such feedback from those least like ourselves, those who are less like a mirror of us. Perhaps it would be best to ask for feedback from those whom we suspect aren't very favorable to us. They may be able to see us through fewer filters.

Giving feedback to participants while very important is also fraught with perils for those who lack skills in this area. It is vital that the receiver hears what is being offered and is able to consider it without the baggage that more often than not accompanies feedback poorly given. Feedback must be given in a descriptive, nonjudgmental manner. It must speak to specifics. Merely describe what has happened or been said and the effects it has had or is having on you or the group or both. No sermonizing, please! Feedback should be delivered with obvious sincerity and tact. You will know when it's given correctly because the receiver will be working with the information you have given him or her instead of reacting to how it was given and defending the behavior or comment that prompted the feedback.

Modeling

The ability to model a variety of behaviors will enable the facilitator to provide those persons who learn best from this method to gain a level of achievement they may well not have been able to absent this approach. Modeling takes place when someone acts in such a way that others may emulate that behavior. Many people are able to replicate a behavior once they have had the opportunity to observe it.

Modeling has many uses. It is especially useful for learners who are more likely to learn from what they see demonstrated than by oral instruction, or for those who need or want alternative ways of responding. Gage (1972) insists that "learning through imitation seems to be especially appropriate for tasks that have little cognitive structure" (p. 47). It is also a useful tool to help persons who demonstrate behaviors that cause them or others difficulties and of which they are unaware. Bandura and Walter (1963) identified three kinds of effects from exposing participants to a model: (1) a modeling effect, (2) an inhibitory or disinhibitory effect, and (3) an eliciting effect. Knowles, Holton, and Swanson (1998) offer the following descriptions of the foregoing. They are respectively: (1) The participant acquires new response patterns, (2) the participant decreases or increases the frequency, latency, or intensity of previously acquired responses, and (3) the participant merely receives from the model a cue for releasing a response that is neither new nor inhibited.

The writer has found that some participants may wish to learn and practice new behaviors within the sessions with the help of the group even though the session may not have been devoted to that purpose. This is particularly true in sessions that extend over several days. An agreement between the participant, the facilitator, and the group can yield significant results when managed correctly by the facilitator. The participant must be in full agreement. It is also best that he or she is the initiator of the idea.

Values-Based Facilitation

A phrase coined by Rees (2001), describes the mindset necessary for facilitators in order that they may be able to consistently exhibit the behaviors appropriate to the art of facilitation. Rees insists that facilitators cannot rely solely on facilitation skills and that "they must work at a deeper level of facilitation *values*. That *attitudes, values,* and *beliefs* are at the core of facilitation" (p. 75). She highlights the point that values drive the beliefs that drive the attitudes that drive behaviors. Thus if a person does not value facilitation and its elements, he or she will not likely be able to adhere to the behaviors necessary to carry it out particularly under stressful conditions. For example, if a person does not value free and open dialogue in meetings, it will be indeed difficult for this person to facilitate such sessions. "If, however, a person's behavior is in alignment with his or her core values and beliefs, the behavior will be consistent and genuine even under pressure" (Rees, 2001, p. 76).

Time Management

Perhaps one of the most overlooked elements of facilitation is that of the diligent use of the participants' time. Advance planning should be scrupulously done. Schedules should be kept. Don't drag things out. Side trips can be interesting and enjoyable, but if they are going to extend the session or cause you to have to delete something that was contracted for, it is usually good advice to stay on the tasks as originally designed. There are times you may find it appropriate to renegotiate with the group to allow for changes mid-stream. With adequate planning these times will be minimized. Sessions should begin and end *on time*. There is a well-worn and wise adage that should be remembered and adhered to: *you can let people go early, but never let them go late.* Make sure that equipment works and that you have spare parts (bulbs, cords, adapters, etc.). It is frustrating to your audience when they are kept waiting while someone tracks down a fuse for some piece of equipment. Plan your work and work your plan.

Managing Conflict

Where two or more people are gathered, there is also present the genesis of conflict. Conflicts over facts are easily resolvable. Conflicts relating to values are the most difficult. Ideas, to the extent that they are rooted in values, may present difficulty in proportion to the level of their relationship to values. Mixed-motive conflicts are important to be identified. Understanding the type of conflict helps you as the facilitator in developing strategies for resolution or at least management. For example, a situation where a person wants to prevail or win and does not care if others also win presents one dilemma, whereas the person who wants to win as much as he or she can and wants the other to lose as much as possible presents quite a different challenge. Thus it is quite apparent that a facilitator must have good skills of identification and resolution of varying types of conflicts that are sure to arise between group members as they interact from time to time.

Conflict is a natural occurrence in groups and if properly managed is beneficial to all concerned. This is particularly true when groups are given a task where the structure is low and the task demanding and the members feel come compulsion to complete it. Tuckman's five-stage model (forming, storming, norming, performing, and adjourning) is a helpful tool for facilitators in assisting the participants through the process of group development.

Forming

In this first phase, the *forming* of the team takes place. The team is assembled, learns about, and generally agrees on goals and begins to tackle the tasks. This has also been referred to as the polite stage. You be nice to me and I'll be nice to you.

Storming

During *storming*, the group addresses issues such as what problems they are really supposed to solve, how they will function, and what leadership model they will accept. Team members open up to each other and confront each others' ideas and perspectives. They may become disruptive and highly animated at times. The polite stage is over; the gloves come off. This is a necessary step and one that requires competence in the facilitator. It requires an ability to lead the participants through this stage to the next one. The facilitator must be alert to any significant change in the assignment or condition as it may send the group back to the storming stage or make it more difficult for them to work through it. Some teams may continue to storm even when they are performing.

Norming

At the *norming* stage members begin to find accommodation with each other and decide how they are going to work together and how they will address the task. Agreement on ground rules is usually the basis for the willingness to make the adjustments necessary to work as a group or team. Trust and motivation to complete the task is generated during this phase.

Performing

Some groups get to the *performing* stage, which represents a high-performance team. Here motivation and self-directedness would be the norm.

Adjourning

Adjourning is the stage for teams that have completed their task and the group is breaking up. The facilitator is called upon to understand the dynamics of a dissolving team, particularly when there has been a significant bond developed among the members.

There some who insist that all teams and groups do not go through all of the stages, or in that order. There is also research that asserts that highly structured tasks such as the task involving airline crews are exempt from the stages. In the view of the writer, Tuckman's mode will be in vogue for most of our needs.

Using DVDs

Fortunately for all of us today we have a fair amount of truly high quality DVDs with which we can enhance our presentations. With just a little imagination, they may be even more impactful. Like any other medium, however, they can be overused, used improperly, or used in such a way that they are robbed of their potential. One video after another over a protracted period does little for a learning program no matter how high the quality. Variety is important in creating and maintaining an optimum learning environment. When you choose to use DVDs, the following information or suggestions may prove helpful.

- First and foremost, preview the DVD more than once. First to see what it's about and whether it will fit into the program you have developed and second, to determine if it will provide the information you need to have conveyed and will it do so powerfully?
- Consider the length of the DVD. Is it too long? Do you have to show it all at once, or will it provide more of an impact if you use a stop-start method? Perhaps only a part of the DVD would be sufficient for your needs.

- Can the DVD be used for a purpose other than the stated subject? For example, the subject of the video may be one thing, but snippets of it may be used for a different subject altogether.
- What time is it being shown, and under what conditions?
- Additionally, you should provide a "listening task" for the viewers. What do you want them to look for? Do you want all of the participants to look for or do the same things? It might be more exciting if the group is divided into teams and given different assignments. What will they be told they have to do when the viewing has been completed? They need to know this in advance as it will help them view differently.
- It goes without saying that the participants need not go through the warning about stealing or improper use of the DVD. After all, that was meant for you. The DVD should be cued up prior to the audience being introduced to it.
- When showing a DVD, it is imperative that the size of the viewing screen be sufficient for the size group you are facilitating and the distance from which they will be from the viewing.
- Some thought needs to be given to adding extension speakers of high sound quality. Good quality sound greatly enhances the presentation.

Remember, the best equipment in the world won't be very helpful if you do not know how to use it. All audio-visual equipment is not the same. Therefore you need to take time in advance to study the specific equipment you will be using.

There are full courses on the facilitation of learning experiences. It is recommended highly that anyone who has not already done so will 1) take a course in facilitation, 2) enroll in a training session on facilitation, and 3) read vigorously about the subject.

VI

EVALUATION AND CLOSURE

Evaluation is among the most abused segments of the training process. The manner in which evaluation is treated by many facilitators lead participants to conclude that little serious effort is to be given to this segment of the learning experience. The atmosphere too often prevalent at this point is "the important stuff is over; now let's get out of here!" Some of this is expected considering where evaluation is placed—at the very end, at a time when everyone's mind is centered on leaving. This can be offset considerably by having the participants evaluate after each module instead of placing the entire evaluation at the very end of the learning experience. If multiple days are involved, an evaluation at the end of each day as well as an overall evaluation at the end of the entire program would be a powerful alternative to the usual end-of-session-only practice.

As we begin our discussion on evaluation it is important to note two distinct types: formative and summative. Formative evaluation takes place during the program design and development. Formative evaluation provides information as to how to make the training program better. Summative evaluation takes place at the end and measures what change has taken place among the trainees as a result of the training.

Training evaluation has been defined by Noe (2010) as "the process of collecting the outcomes needed to determine whether training is effective" and he goes on to say that "the evaluation design refers to the collection of information—including what, whether, how, and from whom—that [information] will be used to determine the effectiveness of the training program" (p. 216).

From the foregoing it is easy to say that evaluation, like training in general, is a process. It includes 1) the performance assessment and the separation of those discrepancies that can be corrected through training, 2) the construction of performance objectives, which are stated in outcome terms, 3) a decision as to how you will evaluate and a plan for doing so, and finally 4) the act of evaluation. Throughout this process consideration must be given to who will be involved in reinforcing what learning or performance has been achieved when the individual returns to the workplace. They should also be involved before the fact in helping to define the actual needs as well.

Evaluation applied to the training process should be no less comprehensive than suggested by Tracy and Noe. Serious thought should be given as to just what information is being sought from the evaluation:

- Were the objectives achieved?
- What do facilitators want to know about what the participants have learned and about how well they have learned it?
- What do the facilitators want to learn from the experience that only the participants can tell them?
- What can be done in this design to 1) reinforce learning and 2) encourage participants toward further learning?
- To what extent has the learning experiences been linked to organizational performance needs?

If charged with doing an impact evaluation (measuring what effect the training had on the job):

- What changes in performance have occurred on the job that can be directly attributed to the training?
- What results have the organization experienced that can be directly attributed to the training participants received from this session in particular?
- To what extent have the supervisors of the trainees been involved in the entire process, beginning with the needs assessment, and to what extent have they agreed to share responsibility for transfer?

According to Denova (1979), in order for an evaluation plan to be effective it should cover at least three areas: 1) the assessment of the change in behavior of the participants, 2) an assessment of the degree to which the activities achieved the stated goals, and 3) an evaluation of both the methods used and the personnel using them.

Phillips (1999) provides a five-level ROI framework:

1. *Reaction and Planned Action,* which measures the participant's reaction to the program and outlines specific plans for implementation.
2. *Learning,* which measures the skills, knowledge, or attitude changes.
3. *Job Applications,* which measure change in behavior on the job and specific application of the training material.
4. *Business Results,* which measures the business impact of the program.
5. *Return on Investment,* which measure the monetary value of the results and costs for the program, usually expressed as a percentage (ROI% = net program benefits divided by program costs times one hundred).

Accurate tracking of individual data is necessary for the effective use of the ROI approach (Eitington, 2002). Whatever approach or model is selected, considerable analysis must be done to determine whether or not the model will provide you with what you are looking for. Additionally, you will need to consider what the model itself requires of you in advance in order to yield the best results. Finally, careful planning must be done to assure that all things work together to produce the best possible results from the model selected.

The time set aside for end-of-course evaluation should be sufficient to permit participants to complete the process without feeling rushed or that completing it will punish them by making them stay "extra time." Too many items can be as problematic as too few. The facilitator's behavior is critical at this juncture. The behavior of the facilitator is being read by the participants and conclusions drawn as to just how the facilitator really feels about the evaluation. Often, facilitators are busy during this time "packing up." This behavior certainly sends a signal that may be quite different than you may intend. What has worked for me is packing away things as I finish with them each day. By the end of the final day very little is left. Usually what is left can be carried very easily and unobtrusively.

Some remarks about the evaluation should be given during the opening session. This will go a long way in helping participants believe that it is valued. They should be helped to focus on the process throughout the session with a few reminders. Having the participants engage in personal contracts for learning during the session as well as keeping journals can enhance and reinforce learning and help them more easily focus on what they have learned thus making evaluation easier and more rewarding for them.

The human resource development practitioner is charged with not only encouraging continuous learning throughout life but with modeling it as well. What better way to model learning, and particularly learning through feedback from others, than to do so through this medium. If you are not serious about learning about your performance, don't waste their time asking for the data. If you are, then your questions must be thoughtful and designed to elicit all that is available for you. It is through this medium that we develop. Most of all, don't get defensive when you get comments that aren't exactly flattering. These comments may be the most valuable of all.

Closure

Closure is much like a commencement was meant to be—not an end to anything but rather a transition from one state to another; from learning to application. Graduation did not mean that no further learning was to take place but merely that the principal focus would shift to the application of what was learned.

In the training session, a great deal of energy goes into learning to solve or identify some problem, to improve our competence in some area. Closure is to be used to channel these energies and the focus of the participants toward application. That is after all, the purpose for which they came.

This can be and often is an emotion-provoking segment of the training process. It all too often goes unnoticed by the facilitator. Many of the participants may experience separation anxiety, particularly if it has been an extended and intense session. There are those who regret that they did not do better or did not get more involved or that they may have said something they wish they had not. There are those who are riding the crest of a high, arising from their perception of a very successful event. It is a time for celebration and a time for resolution. It is incumbent upon the facilitator to be sensitive to what is going on in the session and to design or alter the closure experience to take these things into account. This can and should be a powerful experience. Whether or not it becomes one is greatly dependent on the skills and dedication of the facilitator.

VII

ESTABLISHING THE LEARNING ATMOSPHERE

The climate for learning is primarily the responsibility of the facilitator. One of the first things that is done during the session itself is the establishment of a climate that is conducive for the particular session that has been designed for the present group. What is done in this segment of the training experience depends upon what the participants will be doing, whether they are familiar with one another, the subject matter, and so on. If, for example, the participants are going to be working alone during the session, you would not want to have designed activities to create a close interpersonal climate. This would be counterproductive. If the session will require participants to disclose, activities during climate setting should take this into account and thus prepare them, at least partially, for such experiences.

Generally this segment of the session is begun with the use of one of two types of activities: ice breakers or session openers. Eitington (2002) cautions us to differentiate between ice breakers and session openers. "Both icebreakers and openers are start-up activities that can help participants ease into the learning program. Icebreakers are relatively subject-matter free, whereas openers relate directly to the contents (subject-matter) of the session, course or program" (p. 2). Which to use or whether to use both depends upon various factors, among them, do they know each other? Is the climate already conducive for the session? Are they ready for the introduction of the subject matter? Eitington (2002) insists that whichever you use it reveals the following about you:

- Your philosophy of learning
  - "Your style of training
  - Your attitude toward participants as learners
  - Your anxiety level" (p. 2)

The amount of time allotted for the overall session is also a factor. While climate is important, there has to be sufficient time left for the content of the session as after all that is the reason the session is being held.

Silberman (1990) describes three things that start-up exercises are designed to accomplish:

1. Group building—helping participants to become acquainted with each other and creating a spirit of cooperation and interdependence.
2. On-the-spot assessment learning about the attitudes, knowledge, and experience of the participants.
3. Immediate learning involvement—creating initial interest in the training topic (p. 39).

Silberman also points out that whether we design separate exercises for each of these goals or combine two or more of them depends in large measure on which ones are needed, the time allotted for the entire session, and so on.

Most persons engaged in the delivery of training at the beginning level are familiar with the first goal Silberman offers—namely, group building. It is important that we are as skillful in recognizing the need and value of the other two. For example, it would be lovely indeed if we could always do the type of assessments we would like. For the most part we know far less about the actual participants than we would like. We may have completed a random sampling of the training population, back-up surveys, and the like, yet there are always a significant number of unknowns about the group in front of us. Therefore, Silberman's number-two examples would greatly enhance our chances of adjusting on the spot to the specific needs of the instant group. In the beginning learning exercises, participants may be asked questions about the subject matter, to engage in activities without prior instruction, or to pursue other such activities, suggests Silberman, in an attempt to draw the participants into the session quickly.

Although this segment, Establishing the Learning Atmosphere, is the first thing the participants experience during the actual session, it should not be first in the design phase. Actually it is recommended by the writer that it be designed next to last so that the actual learning experiences may serve as a guide in helping determine just what type of climate-setting experiences will be most appropriate.

Most persons do not come to a session ready to proceed. If there are those who are, there are enough of those who aren't that negatively affect the learning climate. Some participants find it necessary to spend time getting to know others. Some need to let others know who they are, share their credentials, and find out more about the group so that they may make estimates as to what they may expect to gain from those present. Additionally, some need a good read on the composition of the group to determine what their own level of participation will be. Yet still others have not left their place of employment; their bodies may be present but their minds aren't. We can never leave out another very important segment: those who were "told" or "strongly recommended" to come. Perhaps there is serious disagreement over the site, or there is the pending "reorganization." There is the sick child, the plumbing problem, and a host of other concerns, the variety of which defies enumeration. All of these things affect the climate or learning atmosphere. While you will not know everyone's particular issue or problem, if you want the participants' attention, you will have to provide some activities or combination of activities to build the climate through which frustrations may be ameliorated if you expect to have an opportunity for optimum involvement.

In seeking to overcome the kinds of conditions arising from the foregoing, there is one question that I always include in one form or another: "How do you feel about being here?" I usually have them discuss this question in small groups so that they can feel more disposed to express their true feelings. I will ask them to select a reporter and share with the larger group. Since they do not have to identify who said what, some rather interesting comments are usually shared. The facilitator absolutely must model acceptance of their comments as he or she has invited them. Since that is not the only question they are given to discuss and report on, and since it is first on the list to be reported, the small-group report ends with more substantive and positive responses. The important fact to remember is that the responses are going to be controlled by the task questions, which are in the hands of the facilitator.

Personality types also play a major role in how participants come to a session and thus influence the way facilitators may have to adjust their approach to a given situation. For example, people motivated by task are usually more demanding on getting to the meat of the task immediately and are less interested in "warm-ups." Persons motivated by relationships are strong advocates for warm-ups, "getting to know you" type activities, first. People who are direct are not very tolerant of indirect language, thus setting up possible conflict situations with those who are indirect and who find direct language offensive. There are a host of other personality variables that need to be taken into account as activities are designed or selected to establish the proper learning atmosphere as well as maintain it throughout the group's time together.

The climate-setting module provides an opportunity for the facilitator to offset the aforementioned potentially troublesome aspects and help the learners focus on the session itself. These climate issues must be worked through or the atmosphere will not be conducive to learning. Many sessions fail because the facilitator did not establish an appropriate learning atmosphere. Often inexperienced facilitators will rush through this phase, if indeed they deal with it at all, to "get to the good stuff." Some assume that the participants are ready simply because they may have responded to some humorous intervention, and still others are partial to the view that "adults don't need this kind of stuff." The experienced facilitator knows that until this segment of the design is successful, there is little point in proceeding.

Once an appropriate climate has been set, it cannot be forgotten for the rest of the session. Climate must be continually monitored, as there are many things that can and probably will affect it during the course of the overall session. There are things that may occur during the session and things that may occur outside the session that the facilitator may have to cope with. If it is a residential session, participants may get a disturbing telephone call. They may not be accustomed to being away from home at night, particularly if they have small children; they may have an ill family member. Some may not be accustomed to the freedom of being "away," especially without spouse or family members, and they may abuse their evening freedom. If it is not a residential session, events at home may interfere when they return home in the afternoons. The greatest culprit of nonresidential sessions is the return to the office to "check on things." An equally disruptive culprit that is quickly claiming the number-one position is the cell phone. It would be wise to establish rules early on about how this nettlesome problem may be at least minimized. I have in some cases handled this in the planning stage with the client. Notices of the agreement were sent out in with other advance materials regarding cell phone usage. This has worked well, particularly when the CEO has signed on to the policy. Facilitators must be keenly observant in order to detect trouble spots.

Some time must be spent initially each morning (and sometimes after lunch) to get a feel for where people really are. Simply put, climate is a full-time job. It is not a discrete task that once it's completed, you're done. Therefore, pay attention!

Finally, something must be said concerning the impact of group composition on the ability of participants to evolve through this stage. How individuals feel about themselves and how they feel about themselves in the presence of particular others has an impact on their comfort and sometimes on their confidence and their self-respect. This may well be a factor when there are significant differences in status and may arise more often than expected in multicultural sessions. The facilitator must be sensitive to various cues that may be warning signs of difficulty. It is incumbent upon the facilitator to conduct the group in such a way that perceived inequities are minimized if not eliminated and that there is an air of comfort that allows all members to feel free to participate.

Whether we come to a session of our own free will or we have little choice, all of us are faced with assessing the probability of finding our comfort levels within any new group. Schutz (1967) speaks about three issues that must be dealt with when two or more people come together: inclusion, control, and affection. If the facilitator understands this process, then he or she will be able to provide interventions that are appropriate and that are congruent with the particular issue with which the individual or group is engaged at the moment.

Schutz explains that each of these issues brings about different behaviors by the individual. Said another way, persons will behave in a way that is compatible with how well they have resolved their needs with whatever issue is instant. "Since the inclusion involves the process of formation, it usually occurs first in the life of the group" (p. 120). Participants have to decide whether they want to form or belong to a particular group. Schutz explains that control problems usually follow those of inclusion, and while the issues of interaction in the inclusion stage are one of *encountering*, in the control stage the issues of interaction become *confrontation*. One of the major concerns here is power and influence. Some people have a high need for power, while others do not. Some people confront easily, while others had really rather not. Persons engaging in issues of how one truly feels about himself or herself regarding their acceptability on a deeply personal level are engaging in problems of affection. Lovability is one of the main concerns according to Schutz. It is the last and probably the most difficult of the issues. Trust arises from satisfaction of this issue.

Each person comes to an interaction with another with varying needs in each of the issues Schutz raises. Their behaviors will be directly related 1) to how well they are able to find their needs met irrespective of the level they possess and 2) to how well they have resolved their own personal struggles with these issues in their lives. We of course are not therapists, and therefore the latter is not within our purview, but the former is. We need to understand how this relates to comfort levels within the group and what we should or should not do given specific situations. It is also well to note here that these issues are rarely universally settled, especially the affection issues. Whenever there is a significant change in the relationship(s), the cycle begins again. The facilitator must be sensitive to incidents that may affect the level of comfort in the relationships within the group.

Today, all of us are faced with a fast-paced, complex, and ever-changing environment at work and in our private lives. In our busy and often frenzied pace, we seldom have "phase-in" time before leaving one life scene and entering another. We arrive at meetings still psychologically involved with the last event of the day or something that has happened to us in transition. As participants, we are then acted upon by someone in the front of the room that has an agenda for us and who expects us to be totally open to that agenda. We are not there. It is this segment of the learning program, Establishing the Learning Atmosphere, that has the primary responsibility to bring and keep the participants' mind and body at the same place, preferably in the session. To the extent we do this, we will have gone a long way to assure the success of the experience for the participants and the facilitator(s).

VIII

ESTABLISHING THE LEARNING CONTRACT

It is well settled that adults learn best when they have a perception of control over what they are to learn. Certainly no one with a serious mind would disagree that knowing what is to be learned is essential to the learning process. Thus, this segment allows the facilitators to gain "buy-in" from the participants. In some cases the participants have been involved in the assessment of the learning needs. In such cases a simple reminder of that fact is usually sufficient.

More often than you might expect, the particular participants seated before you may well not have been involved in the planning for the training and haven't the foggiest notion as to why they are there. Participants are often sent with little more than "you need to go." In such cases you may well have a lot of hostility, confusion, and frustration to deal with. An alert facilitator should pick this up during the climate-setting phase, in which case it would be handled there, or at least some of it would be. In this module, as said earlier, you need to have them buy into the session; to have them decide that they want to be present whether they originally wanted to be or not. You will need to have them decide that they want to learn what is being offered, or most of it; that it is relevant to them. Remember, the objective is to first get them to decide that they will locate their minds in the same place their bodies happen to be, to decide to be totally present. Absent that nothing of consequence happens.

There are many methods to gain support or buy-in for learning goals. One caveat is in order here. Never give adults a choice unless 1) there is a choice and 2) you are willing to be bound by the choice they make. For example, you could share the objectives with the group and then ask, "Will these meet your needs?" The group then responds in unison, "No."

Then what? It would appear to be a reasonable conclusion, at least to the writer, that any attempt to conduct the session is not likely to be met with much cooperation. Thus, a better question would be "In what ways will this benefit you in your present position?"

Where possible, it would be advisable to divide the participants into small groups, have them select a reporter, and have them respond before the total group. If the groups are developed by a random method, this will be more effective in gaining an acceptance of the proposed agenda and a greater willingness to proceed.

It is equally important in this module and in the climate-setting module that persons feel sufficiently comfortable to be at least reasonably candid. This is vital in efforts to drain off resistance and hostility as well as gaining the buy-in a successful learning experience depends on.

This is also the module where expectations are clarified and a structure is provided for the participants. That is to say, here we explain how the session will be conducted, the types of activities, and so on. This is particularly important if there is anything unusual about the design or in cases where the participants have not been accustomed to either training or the type that is being conducted.

Standards for the session are also developed during this module. I have had many students resist this segment, insisting that adults do not have to be told how to conduct themselves. Ground rules for sessions are extremely important and can actually save a session. Most of us have ways of behaving that are perfectly fine in our everyday professional and private enterprises. However, in working in a group, those same behaviors can be seriously disruptive.

An additional benefit of having the group establish the ground rules or standards is that you are not as likely to have to deal with individual participants around the issue of conduct, thus reducing the possibility of injuring the relationship between you the facilitator and the participants at large. Since everyone is responsible for the enforcement of the contract, you are not left alone with this responsibility. Additionally, when you do have to confront someone, you can simply point to the contract as the intervener, thus possibly avoiding more difficult confrontations.

There are many methods available for this purpose. The writer has used one over the years (or some variation thereof) with sound results. The facilitator writes at the top of a flip chart "Contract." The facilitator then asks the learners to share those behaviors that would be most helpful in creating and maintaining a good learning environment. If the group is hesitant he or she might offer a suggestion such as "not cutting people off." This would be written on the chart in the first person as "I will not cut people off." The facilitator continues to elicit offerings until the group has given all that they have. These become the standards (see example in chapter X).

As with the activities to achieve the learning atmosphere, the writer also recommends that this segment be developed after you have completed the learning activities. It should be designed *after* you have selected the activities to set the climate that permits a smoother flow and can include activities that continue building the climate.

These two segments, Establishing the Learning Atmosphere and Establishing the Learning Contract, are vitally important elements of the design. Your skill in design and implementation of these two will greatly enhance your ability to deliver the learning content for which your client engaged your services, and of course, a satisfied client generally means a high probability of referrals for additional opportunities to provide your services.

IX

PUTTING IT ALL TOGETHER: A SAMPLE DESIGN

As indicated in Section VIII, provided here is a sample of a scripted design. It is intended for demonstration of a scripted format only and should not be considered for any other purpose. The instructions of the facilitator to the participants are in **bold**. Notes to the facilitator are in *italics*. Times indicated are arbitrary.

Terminal Objective

Given a one-day learning experience in constructing performance objectives, participants will construct a performance objective that meets all of the criteria presented by the facilitator during the session without assistance. The level of acceptable performance (criteria/standard) will be determined by the facilitator and the group.

Enabling Objective #1

As a result of 1 1/2 hours of instruction on measurability in writing performance objectives, given three training needs participants will construct measurable performance objectives for each in accordance with the criteria presented during the class by the facilitator without reference to notes. The level of acceptable performance will be determined by the facilitator.

Enabling Objective #2

After a 1 1/2-hour learning experience on writing criteria in performance objectives, participants will construct two performance objectives that are measurable and state the levels of acceptable performance that meet the criteria established during the session without reference to notes. The level of acceptable performance will be determined by the facilitator.

Enabling Objective #3

Given a 1 1/2-hour learning experience on restrictions in performance objectives, participants will construct a performance objective that is measurable and states the level of acceptable performance and any conditions or restrictions under which terminal competency will be demonstrated. Participants may not refer to notes but may confer with one another. The level of acceptable performance will be determined by the facilitator and the group.

Enabling Objective # 4

Given one hour of review on all of the elements of a performance objective, participants will construct a performance objective that states the performance, the standard, conditions, and who or what will confirm that the level of acceptable performance has been demonstrated. Participants may not refer to notes or confer with their colleagues. The level of acceptable performance will be determined by the facilitator.

Establishing the Learning Atmosphere

15 minutes

Participants are greeted by the facilitator and asked to introduce themselves and share how they feel about being at the session and to share their experiences, good and not so good, with writing objectives.

Some may say that they have never written an objective before and therefore have no experience. Some present may well never intend to write any after the session either. They may have little or no control over being in the session, as participants are often sent by someone and against their will.

It will be highly useful to help them see the relevance of the information to be presented to their everyday experience. This example may be helpful to them:

In giving written assignments to subordinates, to our children for that matter, the same elements that are important in constructing objectives are also important. The recipients need to know in specific terms what we want them to do, how well we want them to do it, and under what conditions they must do it. For example, will they have help or will they have to do it alone? They also want to know by when they must do it.

This gives you an excellent lead-in to the next phase in the session where buy-in is to be achieved.

One of the options available to us in getting the above information across without simply telling the participants would be to simply ask the group to give you the most important elements to be included in instructions to a son or daughter concerning a chore that you want them to do around the house. With some facilitation, the same information needed for a performance objective could be elicited. This would, in general, be preferable to simply telling them. Wherever possible, every effort should be made to elicit information from the group, as it has a tendency to improve the sense of self-worth within the membership. This approach would also provide for greater participation by members of the group. Generally, participants are active when in their back-home setting. One of the drawbacks to learning sessions for many is that they cease to be actors themselves and become acted upon; they sit for inordinately long periods being spoken to and not being able to engage in any meaningful two-way communication.

Establishing the Learning Contract

15 minutes

The facilitator shares the objectives for the session, which have been prelisted on flip chart sheets (placed on the wall after sharing so that they are visible throughout the session) and asks the participants to respond to the following question: **How will learning to write behavioral objectives correctly help you professionally and personally?**

Facilitator listens attentively and responds appropriately.

The facilitator then moves to the flip chart and writes across the top of a blank page the word "**Contract.**" *The facilitator tells the group:* **You have an opportunity now to establish a contract for the standards, the guidelines that both you and I** (*"we" if more than one facilitator*) **will adhere to during the session. In other sessions you have attended there may have been things that occurred or behaviors exhibited that you found disturbing or even offensive. You have experienced others that contributed positively to the learning environment. Share those behaviors that you feel need to be demonstrated and those that should not be exhibited during the session.** *If they are not sure of what is being asked for at this point, the facilitator may offer one, such as,* **"We should listen to each other; do you agree?"** *After the group agrees, the facilitator writes the offering in the first person:* "**I will listen.**" *Each offering from the group members is written in the first person. During the offering process no editing is permitted, only clarification. The editing comes when all offerings have been made.*

When the list is exhausted, the facilitator then goes down each item on the list and asks, **"Can we all support this?"** *If the answer is yes, then a check is placed by the item and it is considered included for the session. If the group rejects an item, it is lined out. The facilitator then asks:* "**Who is responsible for the enforcement of the contract?**" *The group will probably eventually respond that everyone is responsible. If not, then the facilitator announces that all are responsible. The contract is then placed on the wall in a conspicuous* *place and remains there throughout the* session. *Participants are encouraged to assist in maintaining compliance by reminding each other when they are in violation. They merely have to state, "Contract." They may point out the specific provision if they wish.*

Activities to Achieve the Performance Objectives

15 minutes—Participatory Theory Presentation

Facilitator gives a theory presentation on performance objectives including the following:

Performance objectives serve as roadmaps for the learner. They are particularly important to adults who need more control over their learning than youthful achievers. If one knows specifically what he or she is to learn in advance, it is easier to learn it. Performance objectives are important to the learning specialist or facilitator as well in that they clearly define what must be taught if the learners are to be able, for example, to perform a particular task.

There are at least three essential elements required in performance objectives. First they must be measurable or observable in some way. Something must occur that lets us know that the person has learned what he or she was intended to learn. They must do something or say something or some combination of both that lets us know that learning has occurred. If our intent was to teach information about objectives, then we could have the participants list, write, recall, recite, describe, and so on.

The choice of words used in performance objectives becomes very important to us as we seek to maintain specificity. If we say that participants will increase their knowledge, then how will we measure knowledge? If the participants "list" the essential elements of an objective that they were not able to list before they came to the session, then we know that they know what we wanted them to know. We know that their knowledge has increased.

A performance objective includes the specified period of the instruction. This could be hours or days. For example, [*facilitator writes each example in quotations on flip chart*] "Given two hours of instruction on . . ." or "Given a two-hour learning experience . . ." It could as well be written, "At the end of two hours of instruction . . ." "As a result of a two-hour learning experience . . ." and so on. The important thing is making sure the elements are there and not whether the way it is stated will get you a PhD in English.

Now let us see if we can tie the specific period of the instruction to the measurability requirements. Let us assume that our session is as this one, to train persons to write measurable objectives. We might then ask ourselves three questions. Perhaps the first one logically would be what do they need to know in order to write measurable objectives. This would be in the cognitive domain.

There are three domains; the cognitive domain has to do with knowing. We will discuss the other two subsequently. It stands to reason that if the objective must be measurable, the words utilized should also be measurable. What are some of the things that participants could do that would let you know that they know which words are measurable and which ones are not? They could list them, recite them, recall them, and so on.

The next question would be what do they need to be able to do? What skill do they need to do this? This would be included in the second domain, the psychomotor domain, which relates to skill. Skills must be demonstrated in some way before we can consider them as being measurable.

The third question is in the affective domain, which deals with attitudes, feelings, values, and beliefs. Thus, what attitudes, feelings, values, and beliefs would be most helpful in writing behavioral objectives?

For this session's purposes we will only deal with either the cognitive or psychomotor domain. We will also concentrate on the elements of the objective.

It is important to briefly mention here that there are also *terminal objectives* and *enabling objectives*. Terminal objectives describe the end result. The enabling objectives represent those things that must be mastered to achieve the end result. The total of the enabling objectives equal the terminal objective. Both terminal and enabling objectives must be measurable and state the level of acceptable performance and conditions and/or restrictions under which the learners must demonstrate terminal competency.

You will not be asked, during this session, to be concerned with whether or not you are constructing a terminal or enabling objective, merely that you are learning to construct a complete performance objective. We will, however, be concerned with whether or not it is in the appropriate domain.

The facilitator elicits several responses from the group and makes an assessment as to whether or not they have enough information to try writing objectives in small groups. If the conclusion is no, more information is provided after an assessment as to specifically what information is needed. If the answer is yes he or she moves to the following assignment.

30 minutes—Small-Group Assignment

The facilitator divides the participants into three roughly equal small groups and assigns the following task:

"Here is a list of three training needs for which you as a group are to write a measurable objective for each:

1. **Giving and receiving feedback**
2. **Decision making**
3. **Problem solving**

You may not look at your notes. Please write your objectives on flip chart paper. You have thirty minutes for this task. Select someone to act as reporter for the group and be prepared to present and defend your objective(s) when called upon to do so."

45 minutes—Small-Group Reports and Critiques

The facilitator advises the group when the time has expired. It may be useful to warn the participants when the end is near, when there are five or ten minutes remaining. The facilitator asks for group reports, allowing groups to volunteer (if no one volunteers, the facilitator designates the order of the group reports). The reporters are instructed to place their objectives either on a flip chart stand or on the wall in front of the class where all members may have a clear view before they proceed. The facilitator tells the rest of the class members that they are to offer feedback to the group as to their objectives' measurability.

If it is measurable, explain why they think so. If it is not, why not, and what could they do to make it so. Any necessary adjustments to the objectives are to be made during this process. The facilitator leads the group to a decision as to the domain in which their objective belongs.

When all groups have been adjudged to have acceptable objectives (objectives that meet the criteria established for measurability), they are posted around the walls.

10-minute break

10 minutes—Theory Presentation: The Level of Acceptable Performance

Consider the following scenario: you have just instructed your teen-age heir to your millions, to "mow the grass." You have given him or her a specified period in which to do it. When the time is up you evaluate the results. There are numerous narrow strips of grass that have not been touched. The flowers in the three little circles have been demolished. The grass clippings are all over the walk. The question for you is "did the heir to your fortune meet the objective?" *The facilitator solicits answers from the participants. There will probably be both yea and nay responses. The facilitator shares that* **yes, the objective was in fact met. The heir "mowed the lawn." For those who would argue that it was not met, they are arguing about the next element of a behavioral objective, "the level of acceptable performance," criteria, or standard. They all mean the same thing.**

How well must I perform the task that I am being asked to perform is the question that goes directly to the performance level required, the quality of my performance. There was no such requirement in the objective given the "heir," merely "mow the lawn."

The facilitator entertains any questions the group may have. The facilitator reminds groups to keep in mind the domain of the objective and should questions arise in that regard they may consult with him or her during their assignment. (The facilitator is to keep in mind that time does not permit participants to concentrate on domains; therefore help in this area should be given liberally so that they may focus on the main tasks.)

20 minutes—Small-Group Assignment

We have now briefly visited two of the elements necessary to be included in a performance objective. During the next assignment we will practice putting them together. Select two of the previous training needs you have been given and construct behavioral objectives for them that are measurable and state the level of acceptable performance. You have twenty minutes for this task. Again, select a reporter, place your final drafts on flip chart paper, and be prepared to report to the large group when called upon to do so. *The facilitator closely but unobtrusively observes the groups to determine where they may be having difficulties and to determine what may need greater attention during small-group critiques later.*

20 minutes—Small-Group Reports and Critiques

Now that we understand the first two elements, let us visit our promising "heir" again. This time you do so with added confidence. You know how to tell him or her what we want in measurable terms, as you know how to describe the level of acceptable performance so that you won't have the lousy results you had last time. So you give your instructions in a fashion that satisfies these two elements. Sometime later you observe the results and are astounded.

What a professional job. Never has your yard looked so good. And then, the rest of the story. Three days later you get a bill from the Yardly Landscaping Co. for $450. It appears that your "heir" wanted to make certain that the job satisfied your criteria; particularly since you emphasized that you were having a lawn party and have invited some rather influential business prospects. So he hired the company to assist him. Did he "do the right thing given the instructions?"

After some discussion the facilitator provides that, speaking strictly from the standpoint of a behavioral objective, the "heir" was perfectly free to ask for assistance since there were no conditions or restrictions given as to how he was to perform. Thus the third element of a performance objective: conditions and/or restrictions under which terminal competency is to be demonstrated. Said another way, the conditions and/or restrictions under which the learners must show us that they have learned whatever it is that they were to have learned and are able to list it, tell it, and so on at the level of quality stated in the objective.

If the learner is to perform a skill, under what conditions or restrictions must it be demonstrated? For example, if the objective deals with handling calls under pressure, then the participants may have to perform in a situation where pressure is simulated. If participants are to learn a set of instructions, then they may have to *recite the instructions without reference to notes, conferring with or being prompted by anyone.* If I am being asked to learn something in a classroom or in a training environment, I need to know what specifically I am to learn, how well I must learn it, and under what conditions I will have to show you that I know it. If I know this in advance, it is easier for me to apply myself toward achieving the learning objective. Are there any questions about conditions or restrictions?

20 minutes—Small-Group Assignment

After responding to any questions, participants may have had the facilitator assigns the following task: Now that you have the third element of a performance objective, select one of the needs you have been given and construct a performance objective that is measurable and states the level of acceptable performance and any conditions and or restrictions under which terminal competency must be demonstrated. You have twenty minutes for this task. As in the other assignments, select a reporter, place your objective on flip chart paper, and be prepared to present to the group when called upon to do so.

15 minutes—Small-Group Reports and Critiques

The facilitator calls for small group reports. Participants critique each objective and provide feedback as to whether or not it meets the criteria for measurability, level of acceptable performance, conditions, and/or restrictions.

When all objectives have been adjudged to have met the criteria, the facilitator then shares that there is yet one more thing to consider.

Revisiting the "heir's" assignment, if we were to give him or her the assignment again, who would observe in some way, whether or not he or she did in fact 1) mow the lawn, 2) mow it in accordance with the established criteria/standard we set, and 3) under the conditions or restrictions required by the objective? In the case of a training session, it could be the facilitator, it could be the group itself, it could be a combination of the two, or it could be a third party. Whoever is designated to fulfill this requirement becomes responsible for determining whether or not the level of acceptable performance has been met. This is a necessary designation. Discuss among yourselves who will fulfill this requirement for you and then add this information to your objective, thus completing its requirements for our purposes during this session. You have four minutes for this task.

10 minutes—Wrap-Up Theory Presentation and Review

When the participants have completed the assignment the facilitator presents a brief summary of the entire session.

During this session we have covered five elements that should be included in a performance objective. We have learned that a performance objective should:

1. Specify the time period the training is to cover.
2. Be measurable.
3. State the level of acceptable Performance.
4. State any conditions and/or restrictions under which the learning is to be demonstrated.
5. Designate who will determine when the performance requirements have been met.

We have also discussed other areas related to writing objectives. Our objectives for this session were as stated in the beginning. (*Facilitator reads the objectives for the day from the flipchart that was read during the first part of the session.*) If you would improve your skills in writing objectives, practice is a must. There are many helpful, easy-to-read books that will help you in furthering your writing skills. Your local library holds a veritable gold mine of opportunities. The best teacher of a skill, however, is practice! Practice! Practice!

Evaluation

25 minutes

Facilitator asks group to **select a recorder and as a group evaluate the session covering at least the following:**

- **Did the session achieve the objectives?**
- **On a scale of 1 (low) to 7 (high), rate the overall session.**
- **What was most helpful? Least?**
- **On a scale of 1 (low) to 7 (high), rate the facilitator and explain your rating.**
- **Add any additional comment you care to make.**
- **When you have finished, call the facilitator back into the room and present your conclusions. You have twenty minutes for the total task.**

After the participants have made their presentation, the facilitator thanks them for their work during the session and their comments, makes a brief appropriate comment, and dismisses the group.

As stated before, this design was for the purpose of providing a simple example of the format spoken to earlier. It was not intended as a model design for content. It was meant only to show how a design might appear in a scripted fashion. The writer hopes that the intended purpose has been accomplished. As you begin to design, you will find many additions to be incorporated; for example, a materials list, having icons in the margins to guide audiovisual prompts, facilitator notes, and the list goes on.

X
A PERSONAL WORD FROM THE AUTHOR

When you begin a learning experience, you are about to embark on one of the most exciting ventures in the human experience that you can imagine. If you like people, find them interesting, and enjoy learning from them and creating experiences through which they may learn, you're about to have a blast. You will get to go to some of the most unusual places filled with some of the most memorable people who will enrich your life beyond measure. Dive in with full abandon. Go for total immersion. Don't hesitate.

Dewitt Jones, in his video *Celebrate What's Right with the World*, tells the story of a famous Scottish weaver whom he had asked what she thought about when she wove. Her reply: "When I weave I weave." The message was clear: whatever you chose to do, do it with all you've got. The returns: a richer life, a more fulfilling life, and a host of people who have the same.

BIBLIOGRAPHY

Anstey, E. A. (1978). A 30 year follow up of the cssb procedure, with future. *Occupational Psychology, 51*, 149-159.

Bandura, A., and Walters, R.H. (1963) Social learning and personality development. NY: Holt, Rinehart, and Winston.

Bellman, G. M. (1980) The consultant's calling: Bringing who you are to what you do. San Francisco: Jossey-Bass.

Bertcher, H. J. (1979). *Group participation: Techniques for leaders and members.* Beverly Hills, CA: Sage.

Blanchard, K., Zigarmi, P., & Zigarmi, D. (1990*). Leadership and the one minute manager: Instructor's guide.* San Diego, CA: The Ken Blanchard Companies.

Block, P. (2011). *Flawless consulting: A guide to getting your expertise used* (3rd ed.)San Francisco: Jossey-Bass.

Brookfield, S. D. (1995). *Becoming a critically reflective teacher.* San Francisco: Jossey-Bass.

Brookfield, S. D. (1996). Breaking the code: aging practitioners in critical analysis of adult educational literature. In R. Edwards, A. Hanson, & P. Raggatt (Eds.), *Boundaries of Adult Learning* (pp. 57-81). New York: Routledge.

Cole, J. (1996). *Beyond prejudice.* Ellenburg, WA: Growing Images.

Cranton, P. (1996). *Professional development as transformative learning: New perspectives for teachers of adults.* San Diego, CA: Jossey-Bass.

Davis, L. N. (1974). *Planning, conducting & evaluating workshops.* Austin, TX: Learning Concepts.

Denova, C. (1979). *Test construction for training evaluation.* New York: Van Nostrand Reinhold.

Dixon, N. M. (1990). *Evaluation: A tool for improving HRD quality.* San Diego, CA: University Associates.

Eitington, J. (2002*). The winning trainer: Winning ways to involve people in learning* (4th ed.). Houston, TX: Gulf Publishing.

Gage, N. L. (1972). *Teacher effectiveness and teacher education.* Palo Alto, CA: Pacific Books.

Hale, J. (2007). The performance consultant's fieldbook: Tools and techniques for improving organizations and people (2nd ed.). San Francisco: Pfeiffer.

Hanson, A. (1996). The search for a separate theory of adult learning: Does anyone really need andragogy? In R. Edwards, A. Hanson, & P. Raggatt (Eds.), *Boundaries of Adult Learning* (pp. 99-108). New York: Routledge.

Harrison, M. I. (1987). *Diagnosing organizations: Methods, models, and processes.* Beverly Hills, CA: Sage.

Horton, M., & Freire, P. (1990). *We make the road by walking: Conversations on education and social change.* Philadelphia, PA: Temple University Press.

Inglis, T. (1997). Empowerment and emancipation. *Adult Education Quarterly, 48*(1), 3-17.

Kanter, R. (1977). *Men and women of the corporation.* New York: Basic.

Karlins, M., & Abelson, H. I. (1970). *Persuasion: How opinions and attitudes are changed.* New York: Springer.

Keil, E. C. (1981). *Assessment centers: A guide for human resource management.* San Francisco: Addison-Wesley.

Knowles, M. L. (1984). *Andragogy in action: Applying modern principles of adult learning.* San Francisco: Jossey-Bass.

Knowles, M. (1989). *The making of an adult educator: An autobiographical journey.* San Francisco: Jossey-Bass

Knowles, M. L. (1992). *The adult learner: A neglected species* (4th ed.). Houston, TX: Gulf Publishing.

Knowles, M. S., Holton III, E. F., & Swanson, R. A. (1998). *The adult learner* (5th ed.). Houston, TX: Gulf Publishing.

Krathwohl, D., Bloom, B., & Masia, B. (1964). *Taxonomy of educational objectives.* New York: David McKay.

Linderman, E. C. (1925). What is adult education? Unpublished manuscript, Butler Library Linderman Archive, Columbia University.

Lusberg, A. (1983). *Testifying with impact.* Washington, DC: Chamber of Commerce of the United States.

Margolis, F. M. (1971). *Training techniques and methodologies.* A hand-out presented at a training session in Maryland on the ADOPT method.

McLaren, P. (1997). Revolutionary praxis: Toward a pedagogy of resistance and transformation. *Educational Researcher, 26* (2), 23-26.

Merriam, S. B., Caffarella, R. S., & Baumgartner, L. M. (2007). *Learning in adulthood: A comprehensive guide 3rd ed.* San Francisco: Jossey-Bass.

Merriam, S. B., Mott, V. W., & Lee, M. (1996). Learning that comes from the negative interpretation of life experience. *Studies in Continuing Education, 18*(1), 1-23.

Mezirow, J. (1990). *Fostering critical reflection in adulthood: A guide to transformative and emancipatory learning.* San Francisco: Jossey-Bass.

Mezirow, J., & Associates. (2000). *Learning as transformation: Critical perspectives on a theory in progress.* San Francisco: Jossey-Bass.

Michalak, D. F., & Yager, E. G. (1979). *Making the training process work.* NY: Harper & Row.

Nadler, L., & Nadler, Z. (Eds.). (1990). *The handbook of human resource development* (2nd ed.). New York: John Wiley and Sons.

Nadler, L. & Nadler, Z. (1994). *Designing training programs: The critical events model.* (2nd. ed.). Houston, TX: Gulf Publishing.

Noe, R. A. (2010). *Employee training and development* (5th ed.). New York: McGraw-Hill.

Pfeiffer, J. W., & Ballew, A. C. (1988a). *Presentation and evaluation skills in human resource development.* San Diego, CA: University Associates.

Pfeiffer, J. W., & Ballew, A. C. (1988b). *Using structured experiences in human resources.* San Diego, CA: University Associates.

Phillips, J. (1999). *Handbook of training evaluation and measurement methods* (3rd ed.). Houston, TX: Gulf Publishing.

Pike, R. W. (1989). *Creative training techniques: Tips, tactics, and how-tos for delivering effective training.* Minneapolis, MN: Lakewood.

Rees, F. (2001). *How to lead work teams* (2nd ed.). San Francisco: Jossey-Bass.

Robinson, D. G., & Robinson, J. C. (1995). *Performance consulting: Moving beyond training.* San Francisco: Berrett-Koeler.

Schutz, W. C. (1967) *Joy: Expanding human awareness.* New York: Grove Press.

Schwarz, R. (2002). *The skilled facilitator.* San Francisco: Jossey-Bass.

Silberman, M. (1990). *Active training: A handbook of techniques, designs, case examples, and tips.* New York: Lexington Books.

Welch, W. A. (1995). Interminority group conflict t. In J. B. Gittler (Series Ed.), *Research in human social conflict: Vol. 1. Racial and ethnic conflict: Perspectives from the social disciplines* (pp. 239-256). Greenwich, CT: Jai Press, Inc.

Welton, M. R. (1995). The critical turn in adult education theory. In M. R. Welton (Ed.), *In Defense of the Lifeworld.* (pp. 11-38). Albany: State University of New York Press.

Wlodkowski, R. J. (1985) Enhancing adult motivation to learn: A guide to improving instruction and increasing learning achievement. San Francisco: Jossey-Bass.